Unifying Against Cyber-Terrorism: A Primer

Phillip J. Wilson

Abstract

Attacks on computer systems for both criminal and political purposes are on the rise in both the United States and around the world. Foreign terrorist organizations are also developing information technology skills to advance their goals. Looking at the convergence of these two phenomena, many prominent security experts in both government and private industry have rung an alarm bell regarding the potential for acts of cyber-terrorism. However, there is no precise definition of cyber-terrorism under United States law or in practice among cyber-security academicians. The lack of a common starting point is one of the reasons existing law fails to directly address cyber-terrorism.

This paper furnishes a lexicon of cyber-related malicious activities and argues for a common working definition of cyber-terrorism. This definition can be both incorporated into current counter-terror legislation and used by government agencies to combat cyber-terrorism. This paper arrives at that definition by analyzing the various definitions proposed by security experts and those in use by governmental organizations. This paper builds on these definitions to arrive at a new definition that is at once broad enough to cover the potentially unique effects of a weapon of cyber-terrorism, while narrow enough to exclude computer network attacks that are relatively minor in nature. Second, analyzing several recent cyber attacks, this paper finds that, while we have not yet faced a "cyber 9/11," computer network attacks for political purposes are on the rise and becoming increasing complex. Third, this paper analyzes current law related to both cyber-crimes and terrorism, finding that while these laws are applicable in many instances, they fall short in adequately focusing on the most important factor when addressing cyber-terrorism: prevention. This paper concludes by recommending that cyber-terrorism, as defined in this paper, be incorporated into some of our most frequently used laws to combat terrorism.

Table of Contents

Introduction

"If I had an hour to save the world I would spend 59 minutes defining the problem and one minute finding solutions" - Albert Einstein

On January 5, 2012, a grand jury sitting in the Eastern District of Virginia indicted seven individuals and two corporations, Megaupload Limited and Vestor Limited, with racketeering conspiracy, conspiring to commit copyright infringement, conspiring to commit money laundering, and two substantive counts of criminal copyright infringement.[1] The indictment was based upon the alleged conspirators' business of profiting from the illegal sharing of copyrighted music and video files by users of their website, megaupload.com.[2] The website was one of the most popular on the Internet, with approximately 150 million registered users, 50 million hits daily, endorsements from music superstars, and earning its founder, Kim Dotcom, $42 million in 2011.[3]

---

[1] U.S. Department of Justice, Office of Public Affairs, *Justice Department Charges Leaders of Megaupload with Widespread Online Copyright Infringement,* FBI Press Release (Jan. 19, 2012), *available at* http://www.fbi.gov/news/pressrel/press-releases/justice-department-charges-leaders-of-megaupload-with-widespread-online-copyright-infringement.

[2] Id.

[3] Nick Perry, *Popular file-sharing website Megaupload shut down,* USATODAY.COM (Jan. 20, 2012), http://www.usatoday.com/tech/news/story/2012-01-19/megaupload-feds-shutdown/52678528/1.

On January 19, 2012, New Zealand police arrived at the mansion of Kim Dotcom by helicopter to arrest him.[4] Mr. Dotcom retreated into a "safe room" where he had stored weapons, including a sawed-off shotgun.[5] The police eventually cut their way into the room where he was arrested.[6] Following Dotcom's arrest, three other indicted co-conspirators were arrested in Auckland, New Zealand at the request of the United States.[7] Additionally, more than 20 search warrants were executed in the United States and eight other countries, seizing approximately $50 million in assets.[8] The action was "among the largest criminal copyright cases ever brought by the United States and directly targets the misuse of a public content storage and distribution site to commit and facilitate intellectual property crime."[9]

In the immediate aftermath of the arrests, one segment of the online community responded with what the New York Times called "digital Molotov cocktails,"[10] and CNET called "going nuclear."[11] The hacker group Anonymous, in apparent dissatisfaction with the Megaload arrests, launched cyber-attacks against the websites of the White House, the U.S. Department of Justice (DoJ), the U.S. Copyright Office, and

---

[4] Ben Sisario, *4 of 7 Named in Megaupload Indictment Denied Bail in New Zealand*, N.Y. Times (Jan. 20, 2012), http://www.nytimes.com/2012/01/21/technology/megaupload-indictment-internet-piracy.html.

[5] Id.

[6] Id.

[7] FBI Press Release, Jan. 19, 2012, *supra* note 1.

[8] Id.

[9] Id.

[10] Sisario, N.Y. Times, *supra* note 4.

[11] Molly Wood, *Anonymous goes nuclear; everybody loses?*, CNET (Jan. 19, 2012), http://news.cnet.com/8301-31322_3-57362437-256/anonymous-goes-nuclear-everybody-loses/ (arguing that the FBI may have goaded Anonymous into attacking their website with the arrests following debates about new legislation on Internet piracy in an attempt to turn public support away from Anonymous and similar hacking groups).

several entertainment companies and trade groups.[12] Across the globe, network attacks

were up 24 percent immediately following the arrests.[13] Anonymous's cyber-attacks were

clearly politically motivated and geared towards influencing both government and

civilian opinion. These actions were definitely crimes, but not motivated by money or

other traditional criminal motives. Should the motivations of such an attack affect how it

is classified under the law? Was this a cyber-crime that should be treated like any other?

Was it an act of civil disobedience? Or, did its political motivations make it a unique form

of terrorism?

Cyber-crimes are now a part of everyday modern life, with estimated losses in 2009

placed at up to $1 trillion globally.[14] Given the potential criminal rewards, they are as

unlikely to be eliminated as age-old crimes such as theft or battery. Lawmakers have

attempted to keep pace with statutes like the Computer Fraud and Abuse Act (CFAA),

which is continually updated and criminalizes almost any crime committed in the United

States conducted through computers or other information systems.[15] However, the

anonymity inherent in the architecture of the Internet has made it easy for criminals to act

in cyberspace without getting caught.[16] This anonymity, combined with society's

---

[12] <u>Id.</u>

[13] <u>Id.</u>

[14] Elinor Mills, *Study: Cybercrime cost firms $1 trillion globally*, CNET (Jan. 28, 2009), http://news.cnet.com/8301-1009_3-10152246-83.html; *See also* Internet Crimes Complaint Center, 2010 Internet Crime Report, *available at* http://www.ic3.gov/media/annualreport/2010_IC3Report.pdf.

[15] 18 U.S.C. §1030 (2006). The CFAA has been amended six times since it became law, in: 1988, 1994, 1996, 2001, 2002, and 2008.

[16] *See e.g.,* Thomas Crampton, *Nigeria to battle Internet scams that taint its image*, N.Y. Times (Jan. 23, 2004), http://www.nytimes.com/2004/01/23/business/worldbusiness/23iht-t16_0.html (reporting on the infamous) Nigerian Internet fraud schemes); *and*

increasing reliance on computers and computer networks have also made possible a new type of cyber-crime with different motivations: cyber-terrorism. There is a growing recognition of the threat of cyber-terrorism, and an ever-increasing amount of proposed legislation and academic thought is being put towards its prevention.[17] A well thought out strategy, however, needs to start with a common working definition of cyber-terrorism.

This paper proposes a common working definition that legislators and government agencies can work from, ensuring that the solutions developed are addressed to the most pressing problems. This proposed definition is broad enough to cover the potentially unique effects of a weapon of cyber-terrorism, while narrow enough to exclude computer network attacks that are relatively minor in nature. The definition is carefully tailored, as a definition that is either too broad or too narrow risks being either irrelevant or useless.

This paper also shows how existing counter-terrorism statutes could be amended to incorporate the proposed definition of cyber-terrorism. Statues included are the material support to terrorism statutes,[18] the Foreign Intelligence Surveillance Act (FISA),[19] conspiracy to kill, kidnap, maim, or injure persons or damage property in a foreign country,[20] and the statutes addressing weapons of mass destruction (WMD).[21] By

---

Somini Sengupta & Jenna Wortham, *U.S. Charges 7 in Online Ad Fraud Scheme*, N.Y. Times (Nov. 9, 2011), http://www.nytimes.com/2011/11/10/technology/us-indicts-7-in-online-ad-fraud-scheme.html (describing a recent Internet fraud scheme that diverted marketing revenue to fraudulent sites by replacing real ads with fraudulent ones).

[17] *See generally* Susan W. Brenner, *"At Light Speed" - Attribution and Response to Cybercrime/Terrorism/Warfare*, 97 J. Crim. L. & Criminology 397 (2007) (describing why current laws do not adequately address the issue of attack attribution); *and* Aviv Cohen, *Cyberterrorism: Are we Legally Ready*, 9 J. Int'l Bus. & L. 1 (2010) (arguing for new international conventions to govern cyber-terrorism).

[18] 18 U.S.C. §§ 2339A-B (2006); 50 U.S.C. § 1701 et seq. (2006).

[19] 50 U.S.C. § 1801 et seq. (2006).

[20] 18 U.S.C. § 956 (2006).

[21] 50 U.S.C. § 2332A (2006).

incorporating cyber-terrorism into these statutes, a body of law that has been effectively used to combat traditional acts of terrorism would become available to the cyber realm. The author does not suggest that these changes, even if enacted wholesale, would eliminate cyber-terrorism as a threat. However, they are examples of how a common definition of cyber-terrorism can be used, and a piece in the puzzle towards the most important aspect of any type of terrorism: prevention.

Part I of this paper examines the current state of cyber threats and why current law is inadequate to deal with cyber-terrorism. Part II aims at providing a definition of cyber-terrorism. Included in this section is an examination of the elements of this definition, a lexicon of definitions used within that definition, an examination of other types of cyber-attacks, and a comparison with current definitions of cyber-terrorism suggested by academics or in use by government agencies. Part III examines several recent major cyber-attacks to determine whether they fit this definition of cyber-terrorism. Part IV of this paper is an overview of current domestic laws relating to both cyber-crimes and terrorism, and a discussion of the major stumbling block in fighting cyber-terrorism: attribution. Part V of this paper discusses incorporation of cyber-terrorism into several current counter-terrorism statutes that could be effectively used to prevent cyber-terrorism.

Part I. The Current Situation

"The very technologies that empower us to lead and create also empower those
who would disrupt and destroy." - 2010 National Security Strategy

Attacks on information systems and networks have increased at an exponential rate

in the last two decades. A 1996 GAO report found that the Department of Defense (DoD)

faced 250,000 attempted attacks on its networks in 1995;[22] in 2006 the number had risen

to 6 million; and in 2008 the number was more than 300 million.[23] Looking beyond the

government, these numbers become staggering. Seventy-four million people in the

United States were victims of cyber crime in 2010, resulting in an estimated $32 billion

in financial losses.[24] This section examines the current threats to information systems and

explores how the current approach is inadequate to the task of preventing a major cyber-

attack on the United States.

---

[22] U.S. General Accounting Office, GAO/AIMD-96-84, Information Security: Computer
Attacks at Department of Defense Pose Increasing Risks 3 (1996).
[23] Scott Hamilton, *Industry pulse: The unknown*, Armed Forces J.,
http://www.armedforcesjournal.com/2009/11/4268936/ (last visited Feb. 4, 2012)
(describing the growing awareness of government and private companies to develop a
robust cyber-security industry).
[24] Norton Cybercrime Report 2011,
http://www.symantec.com/content/en/us/home_homeoffice/html/cybercrimereport/ (last
visited Feb 4, 2012).

A. The Current Threat

President Barack Obama has labeled computer network attacks "among the most serious economic and national security risks we face as a nation,"[25] and that "America's economic prosperity in the 21st century will depend on cybersecurity."[26] These statements, although serious, are tame compared to some fears of cyber-security experts. Leading the charge has been the former chief counterterrorism adviser on the National Security Council, Richard Clarke.[27] In his book "Cyber War," Clarke describes the potential for "a massive cyberattack on civilian infrastructure that smacks down power grids for weeks, halts trains, grounds aircraft, explodes pipelines, and sets fire to refineries."[28] Former Director of National Intelligence and Director of the National Security Agency, Mike McConnell, stated: "The warnings are over. It could happen tomorrow."[29] McConnell described the potential for such an attack as impacting the global economy on "an order of magnitude surpassing" 9/11.[30]

Whether cyber-attacks have the potential to rise to the level just described is certainly debatable.[31] However, the facts indicate that cyber-attacks for reasons other than

---

[25] President Barack Obama, Remarks by the President on Securing Our Nation's Cyber Infrastructure, The White House (2009), http://www.whitehouse.gov/the-press-office/remarks-president-securing-our-nations-cyber-infrastructure.
[26] Id.
[27] *Profile: Richard Clarke*, BBC (Mar. 22, 2004), http://news.bbc.co.uk/2/hi/americas/3559087.stm.
[28] Richard A. Clarke & Robert Knake, *Cyber War: The Next Threat to National Security and What to Do About It* 260 (2010).
[29] Max Fisher, F*mr. Intelligence Director: New Cyberattack May Be Worse Than 9/11*, The Atlantic (Sept. 30, 2010), http://www.theatlantic.com/politics/archive/2010/09/fmr-intelligence-director-new-cyberattack-may-be-worse-than-9-11/63849/.
[30] Id.
[31] *See, e.g.*, Joshua Green, *The Myth of Cyberterrorism* Wash. Monthly (Nov. 2002), http://www.washingtonmonthly.com/features/2001/0211.green.html (arguing the threat of cuber-terrorism is over-hyped and focusing too heavily on cyber-security will have a

money are becoming more and more prevalent. The years 2006 to 2010 saw a 650

percent increase on federal agencies.[32] The rise in politically active hacking groups, such

as Anonymous, demonstrate that the Internet is increasingly a platform for dissenters,

domestic and foreign, to express their disagreement with the government.[33] Espionage on

information systems is rapidly rising as well.[34] Even "air-gapped"[35] classified networks

are not immune, as the DOD's classified network was compromised in 2008 by an attack

using flash drives.[36]

Politically motivated cyber-attacks are not limited to government websites. An

increasing number of attacks target corporations having policies with which hacking

---

negative effect on the information technology industry); *and* Derek E. Bambauer, *Conundrum*, 96 Minn. L. Rev. 584, 612 (2011) (arguing that scenes of cyber apocalypse are overblown, but cyber threats are real and that information, not systems should be the focus of cyber-security); *but see* Richard Clarke, National Coordinator for Security Infrastructure Protection and Counter-terrorism, National Security Council, Keynote Address at the Terrorism and Business Conference: Threats to U.S. National Security: Proposed Partnership Initiatives Towards Preventing Cyber Terrorist Attacks, *in* 12 DePaul Bus. L.J. 33 (1999) (arguing that large scale cyber-attacks are a distinct possibility and that the best way to respond to cyber-threats is through the development of public-private partnerships).

[32] U.S. Gov't Accountability Office, GAO-11-463T, Continued Attention Needed to Protect Our Nation's Critical Infrastructure and Federal Information Systems (2011) (from 5,503 incidents reported in FY 2006 to 41,776 reported in FY 2010).

[33] *See e.g.*, Kukil Bora, A*nonymous Timeline 2011: The Rise of the Hactivist*, Int'l Bus. Times (Feb. 23, 2012), http://www.ibtimes.com/articles/303449/20120223/anonymous-hacking-hactivist-acta-protest-ddos-blackout.htm (charting the increasing rate of hacking by Anonymous).

[34] Ellen Nakashima, *In a world of cybertheft, U.S. names China, Russia as main culprits*, Wash. Post (Nov. 3, 2011), http://www.washingtonpost.com/world/national-security/us-cyber-espionage-report-names-china-and-russia-as-main-culprits/2011/11/02/gIQAF5fRiM_story.html (reporting on an intelligence report to Congress naming China and Russia as the primary culprits of cyber-espionage).

[35] "Air gapped" networks are those physically, electrically, and electromagnetically isolated from other networks such as the Internet.

[36] William J. Lynn III, U.S. Deputy Secretary of Defense, *Defending a New Domain: The Pentagon's Cyberstrategy*, Foreign Affairs (Sept./Oct. 2010), *available at* http://www.foreignaffairs.com/articles/66552/william-j-lynn-iii/defending-a-new-domain (describing defense intitiatives put in place to defend the U.S. from cyber threats).

groups disagree, such as the 2010 attack on Google by a "highly sophisticated and

targeted attack" originating from China,[37] and attacks against the music and motion

picture industries for their support of anti-copyright infringement legislation.[38] Other

attacks have had widespread effects on entire nations, such as the 2007 attack on Estonia

by Russian hacking groups,[39] and the 2009 cyber-attacks against South Korea.[40] (These

attacks are describe in Part III below.)

Every day, new components of our infrastructure are being connected to networks,

allowing more efficient operation, but also opening those components to computer

network attacks.[41] The development of smart grid technology is an example of this. By

placing controls of the power grid on interconnected information systems, power can be

efficiently controlled and distributed. The security of these systems should be made a

---

[37] Andrew Jacobs & Miguel Helft, *Google, Citing Attack, Threatens to Exit China*, N.Y. Times (Jan. 13, 2010), http://www.nytimes.com/2010/01/13/world/asia/13beijing.html (discussing Google's reaction to network attacks it says were aimed at curbing free speech in China).

[38] *See e.g., Attacks target recording industry*, BBC (Sept. 20, 2010), http://www.bbc.co.uk/news/technology-11371315.

[39] *A look at Estonia's cyber attack in 2007*, msnbc.com, http://www.msnbc.msn.com/id/31801246/ns/technology_and_science-security/t/look-estonias-cyber-attack/ (last visited Feb 4, 2012) (the cyber attack on Estonia 2007, discussed in Part II of this paper, was a three week assault on Estonia's "e-government" following the removal of a Russian memorial in Estonia's capital).

[40] *South Korea hit by cyber attacks*, BBC (Mar. 4, 2011), http://www.bbc.co.uk/news/technology-12646052 (these attacks were blamed by the South Korean government on North Korea, but definitive links were never established).

[41] *See e.g.*, Matthew L. Wald, *Making Electricity Distribution Smarter*, N.Y. Times Green Blog (April 21, 2009), http://green.blogs.nytimes.com/2009/04/21/making-electricity-distribution-smarter/ (discussing the spread of smart grid technology that increases efficiency in electrical power operations by monitoring and controlling electricity distribution); *and* Norman Announces New SCADA Security System to Protect Industrial Infrastructure, Market Watch (Feb. 14, 2012), http://www.marketwatch.com/story/norman-announces-new-scada-security-system-to-protect-industrial-infrastructure-2012-02-14 (announcing release of updated security measures for pipeline SCADA systems).

national priority.[42] However, no level of security spending will completely eliminate

vulnerabilities, and those vulnerabilities will eventually be exploited.[43]

The dramatic rise in both attacks and vulnerabilities have led governments to

recognize the enormity of the issue, resulting in a push for increasing mandated cyber-

security covering both government and private networks. At a 2011 hearing, Rep. Dan

Lungren, Chairman of the House Subcommittee on Infrastructure Protection,

Cybersecurity and Security Technologies, stated that one of the top listed concerns for

American lawmakers, intelligence officials and military leaders is the rapidly growing

cyber threat.[44] He cited the belief that a successful cyber attack on our power grid or

communications networks could cripple our economy and threaten national security.[45]

The President has established multiple task forces to evaluate and make

recommendations for the future of cyber-security.[46] British Foreign Secretary William

Hague convened a conference on cyber attacks after criticisms of failing to take cyber

threats seriously in his country.[47] Mr Hague stated a "global coordinated response" is

---

[42] *See generally* Clarke keynote address, *supra* note 31.

[43] *See* Derek E. Bambauer, *Conundrum*, 96 Minn. L. Rev. 584 (2011) (arguing that information, not systems should be the focus of cyber-security).

[44] *Opening Statement at the Markup of H.R. 3674 "Promoting and Enhancing Cybersecurity and Information Sharing Effectiveness Act of 2011: Before the Subcommittee on Infrastructure Protection, Cybersecurity and Security Technologies,* 112th Cong. (2011) (statement of Rep. Lungren, Chairman).

[45] Id.

[46] *See generally* Bill Lane, *Cyber Security and Communications*, Fed. Commc'ns Comm'n, http://www.fcc.gov/pshs/techtopics/techtopics20.html (cataloguing executive branch task forces focused on cyber-security).

[47] *GCHQ chief reports "disturbing" cyber-attacks on UK*, BBC News UK (Oct. 31, 2011), http://www.bbc.co.uk/news/uk-15516959 (following several attacks on UK government and technology firm computers, the UK convened a conference with world leaders and cyber-security experts to discuss a coordinated global response to cyber attacks).

required to combat cyber threats.[48] In 2005, the European Council adopted the European

Program for Critical Infrastructure Protection (EPCIP) to focus on strengthening

information systems, and enhancing preparedness for attacks on critical infrastructure.[49]

If, as suggested by these experts, cyber-attacks that equate to terrorism are possible,

then there are multiple reasons to think terrorist groups will utilize information systems

as weapons of terror. The Internet and other information systems hold every attribute

terrorists might want to achieve their goals. The Internet is global, anonymous, and

allows collaboration by people around the world on a single project.[50] Cyber-terrorism

may be the next logical step in the evolution of terrorism. Given the possibility,

preventive laws should be implemented as soon as possible, not after the first major

attack. Sen. Joseph Lieberman, while introducing the Cybersecurity Act of 2012, stated

his belief that "time is not on our side," and that we should act to prevent a cyber 9/11

before it happens instead of reacting after it happens."[51] Senator Lieberman went on to

describe how he saw the threat in greater detail, stating:[52]

> Every day rival nations, terrorist groups, criminal syndicates and individual
>
> hackers probe the weaknesses in our most critical computer networks, seeking to
>
> steal government and industrial secrets or to plant cyber agents in the cyber
>
> systems that control our most critical infrastructure and would enable an enemy to

---

[48] Id.

[49] *See generally*, European Programme for Critical Infrastructure Protection,
http://europa.eu/legislation_summaries/justice_freedom_security/fight_against_terrorism/
l33260_en.htm (last visited Feb. 20, 2012).

[50] *See generally* Gabriel Weimann, *How Modern Terrorism Uses the Internet*, United
States Institute of Peace, Special Rep. 116 (2004) (identifying eight different ways
terrorists use the Internet to advance their cause).

[51] *Opening Statement of Chairman Joseph Lieberman "Securing America's Future: The
Cybersecurity Act of 2012": Before the Sen. Homeland Security and Governmental
Affairs Committee*, 112th Cong. (2012) (statement of Sen. Lieberman, Chairman).

[52] Id.

seize control of a city's electric grid or water supply system with the touch of a
key from a world away.

What if cyber-terrorist were currently planning a major attack? What laws could be used
to combat this threat? Certainly there are laws on the books, such as the CFAA under
which an attack could be prosecuted,[53] but these laws may be of little consequence in
attempting to prevent such an attack.

B. The Inadequacy of the Current Approach

This paper does not advocate that a cyber-apocalypse is just around the corner; the
author will leave that judgment to intelligence and industrial security experts. However, if
it is even possible, it would be wise to develop a preventative approach. As this paper is
under draft, the Senate Homeland Security and Governmental Affairs Committee are
putting forth a major piece of legislation, the Cybersecurity Act of 2012.[54] This bill seeks
to implement a regulatory structure on critical industry cyber-security and promote
information sharing between private parties and government agencies.[55] Regulatory
oversight, information sharing and significant investment in cyber-security for the
components of our national infrastructure that run on information networks, such as
power grids, pipelines, and systems containing economic data, are all necessary pieces in
the prevention puzzle.[56] However, just as new legal tools for law enforcement and
prosecutors were utilized in the war against terrorism, similar legal tools should be made
available to prevent acts of cyber-terrorism.

---

[53] 18 U.S.C. §1030 (2006) (discussed infra in Part IV of this paper).

[54] Cybersecurity Act of 2012, *available at* http://www.hsgac.senate.gov/.../the-cybersecurity-act-of-2012-s-2105

[55] Id.

[56] *See* Lynn, *Defending a New Domain, supra* note 36.

This is not to say that the traditional law enforcement model has no role to play in catching and prosecuting those who commit cyber-crimes for political reasons. Not all those committing cyber-attacks for political purposes have escaped punishment. Mitchell Frost was sentenced to thirty months in prison following a 2007 attack against conservative political websites such as Ann Coulter and Bill O'Reilly.[57] A college student who hacked Sarah Palin's email account during the 2008 presidential campaign was sentenced to a year and a day in a halfway house.[58] In a successful prosecution of an early cyber-attack on physical infrastructure, an Australian was sent to jail for hacking into a waste management system and dumping millions of liters of raw sewage into park, rivers, and businesses.[59] Perhaps the best example of traditional law enforcement methods was the capture of five Anonymous members in 2012.[60] Following an arrest in 2008, a New York based hacker, Hector Monsegur agreed to assist the FBI in tracking other members of Anonymous in exchange for leniency at sentencing.[61] His cooperation led to the arrests of five prominent members of Anonymous, prompting one cyber-security expert to state: "This is the most important roll-up of hackers ever."[62]

---

[57] Robert McMillan, *Bill O'Reilly hacker gets 30 months*, CSO (Nov. 8, 2010), http://www.csoonline.com/article/634363/bill-o-reilly-hacker-gets-30-months.

[58] Bill Poovey, *Palin e-mail hacker sentenced to 1 year, 1 day*, msnbc.com (Nov. 12, 2010), http://www.msnbc.msn.com/id/40152249/ns/politics-more_politics/t/palin-e-mail-hacker-sentenced-year-day/ (the defendant had hoped to find information in Palin's online accounts that could derail her campaign, but found nothing helpful to that effect).

[59] Tony Smith, *Hacker jailed for revenge sewage attacks,* The Register (Oct. 31, 2001), http://www.theregister.co.uk/2001/10/31/hacker_jailed_for_revenge_sewage/ (the perpetrator worked for the company that installed the waste management controlling software and had been recently rejected for employment by the local city council).

[60] Ellen Nakashima, Peter Finn & Sari Horwitz, *5 members of Anonymous hacking group charged*, Wash. Post (Mar. 6, 2012), http://www.washingtonpost.com/world/national-security/5-members-of-anonymous-hacking-group-charged/2012/03/06/gIQAJ70FvR_story.html?hpid=z4.

[61] Id.

[62] Id.

This type of traditional law enforcement work certainly has its place in combatting cyber-terrorism. However, the overwhelming number of cyber related crimes evade detection or prosecution. There are a number of reasons for this. One is that many large corporations are loath to report the astounding number of attacks they receive.[63] Another is that cyber-crimes continue to receive lower priority attention than traditional crimes.[64] However, the primary reason is that cyber-crimes are extraordinarily difficult to attribute to a particular culprit.[65]

Current cyber-crime laws, when applied to potential acts of cyber-terrorism, also suffer from another aspect of traditional criminal law: relying on prosecution for deterrence and prevention. Traditional criminal law seeks to prevent future crimes primarily through the deterrence of successfully catching and prosecuting criminals. As the head of U.S. Cyber Command, (then) Lieutenant General Keith Alexander, put it:

---

[63] *See* Ellen Nakashima & David S. Hilzenrath, *Cybersecurity: SEC outlines requirement that companies report cyber theft and attack*, Wash. Post (Oct. 20, 2011), http://www.washingtonpost.com/world/national-security/cybersecurity-sec-outlines-requirement-that-companies-report-data-breaches/2011/10/14/gIQArGjskL_story.html (describing new Securities and Exchange Commission guidelines for reporting losses due to computer network attacks to corporation shareholders); *see also* Paul Rosenzweig, *Information Sharing and the Cybersecurity Act of 2012*, Lawfare (Feb. 14, 2012), http://www.lawfareblog.com/2012/02/information-sharing-and-the-cybersecurity-act-of-2012/ (discussing information sharing procedures in the proposed Cybersecurity Act of 2012, designed to overcome corporate hesitancy to share information about CNA); *and* Gus Coldebella, *Cyber Security Act of 2012 requires a liability protection bug fix,* The Hill (Feb. 22, 2012), http://thehill.com/blogs/congress-blog/technology/212049-cyber-security-act-of-2012-requires-a-liability-protection-bug-fix (arguing the information procedures in the Cybersecurity Act of 2012 do not go far enough and open corporations to potential liability).

[64] *See* Ron Condon, *Analysis: How to catch a cyber criminal? Do it yourself,* Sillicon.com (Apr. 24, 2006), http://www.silicon.com/legacy/research/specialreports/ecrime/0,3800011283,39158294,00.htm (arguing that, because police tend to place lower priority on cyber-crimes, companies that are victims of cyber-crimes should pursue cyber-criminals using their own resources).

[65] *See generally* Bambauer, *supra* note 43.

"The bottom line is, the only way to deter cyber attack is to work to catch perpetrators and take strong and public action when we do."[66] However, when making the leap from traditional cyber-crime to cyber-terrorism, the stakes become higher and prevention becomes the most important factor.

Overall, the current focus on cyber-terrorism can be compared to that of terrorism before 9/11. The 9/11 Commission Report noted that the FBI was "case-specific, decentralized, and geared towards prosecution."[67] The report went on to note that "[s]ignificant FBI resources were devoted to after-the-fact investigations of major terrorist attacks, resulting in several prosecutions."[68] The FBI was very good at doing what they had always done, investigate crimes, make arrests and then hand over the perpetrators to the United States Attorney's Office for prosecutions. However, when dealing with attackers that utilize terrorism, after-the-fact prosecution is not an effective deterrent. Other methods of prevention are required to stop terrorist acts, and laws going forward should reflect that priority. However, before a problem can be prevented, it must be defined.

---

[66] Advance Questions for Lt. Gen. Keith Alexander, USA Nominee for Commander, U.S. Cyber Command Before the S. Armed Serv. Comm., 111th Cong. 23 (2010).

[67] 9/11 Commission, Final Report of the National Commission on Terrorist Attacks Upon the United States, Executive Summary 13.

[68] Id.

Part II. Defining Cyber-Terrorism

"As we know, there are known knowns; there are things we know we know. We also know there are known unknowns; that is to say we know there are some things we do not know. But there are also unknown unknowns - the ones we don't know we don't know."

- Defense Secretary Donald Rumsfeld, Feb. 12, 2002

With any great problem, often the first and most difficult step is properly defining it, and cyber-terrorism is no exception. Cyber-terrorism is logically sub-categorized under both terrorism and cyber-crimes. These categories are either relatively new phenomena, as with cyber-crimes, or phenomena that has taken on new historical significance, as with terrorism. The result being the definitions of these categories continue to be unsettled.[69] Regarding cyber-crimes generally, there must be some violation of a criminal code that involves the use of computers or other information systems, usually accomplished through the Internet, but not necessarily.[70] With terrorism, the United States Government offers multiple definitions, and internationally, there is even less clarity on a definition of terrorism.[71]

---

[69] *See* Bruce Hoffman, *Inside Terrorism* (2d ed., Colum. U. Press, 2006) (evaluating the historical development of terrorism and why it is so difficult to define).

[70] *See, e.g.,* 18 U.S.C. § 1030 (2006).

[71] *See* Nicholas J. Perry, *The Numerous Federal Definitions of Terrorism: The Problem of Too Many Grails*, 30 J. Legis. 249 (2004) (Examining twenty-two of the definitions for terrorism in federal lexicon and arguing for a single definition); *see also* United States v. Yousef, 327 F.3d 56, 106 (2d. Cir. 2003) ("We regrettably are no closer now than eighteen years ago to an international consensus on the definition of terrorism, or even its proscription.").

Given the evolving definitions of the broader categories, it is no surprise that definitions of cyber-terrorism have been equally divergent.[72] Additionally, the United States has yet to see a cyber-attack on the level of a major terrorist attack. Without a major event to spark public debate, lawmakers have little incentive to define and address this particular crime. Nevertheless, to develop a legal framework that helps to prevent, deter, and defend against a cyber-terrorist act, the appropriate first step must be to develop a practical working definition that precisely defines what type of attacks should be considered cyber-terrorism.

This section begins by offering a definition of cyber-terrorism that can be used as a common starting point for definitions in U.S. Code, as well as those used by governmental agencies. As this section will demonstrate, the current definitions of cyber-terrorism are widely divergent in the scope of actions that fall under their definition. This divergence makes it difficult to develop common strategies and tactics to defeat cyber-terrorism. This paper does not intend to suggest that all legislations and agency mission statements use the exact same definition of cyber-terrorism. However, these definitions should begin from a common starting point, from which they may be altered to serve the legislative or agency purpose.

This section will also examine a lexicon of terms that are generically used to describe different aspects of cyber-attacks. Using these definitions, this section then categorizes the various types of cyber-attack and explains how they are distinguished from this papers definition of cyber-terrorism. Next, this paper's definition of cyber-

---

[72] *See* Mohammad Iqbal, *Defining Cyberterrorism*, 22 J. Marshall J. Computer & Info. L. 397 (2004) (exploring the different definitions of cyber-terrorism that have been suggested).

terrorism is analyzed in comparison to those in existence, discussing how they differ and

why they should yield in favor of this paper's definition.

A. Proposed Definition of Cyber-Terrorism

Following the attacks of September 11, 2001, terrorist organizations have faced a

full-court press by the United States and other nations who recognize the threat posed to

their national security. Foreign Terrorist Organizations (FTO) such as Al-Qaeda have

responded in part by utilizing the Internet for organizational and propaganda purposes

with on-line publications such as Inspire.[73] The last decade has also seen the rise in

politically motivated hacking groups, both in the United States and abroad.[74] These

groups have become increasingly daring and sophisticated in their attacks.[75] It is logical

to assume that both these types of organizations will eventually attempt to utilize the

Internet and other information systems as an instrument of terror.[76] Utilizing the Internet

as a weapon of terror is inexpensive, anonymous, and global. At the same time, the

United States is becoming more reliant on technology to control our critical

infrastructure, both physical and informational.[77] According to the DoD:

---

[73] Marc Ambinder, *Al Qaeda's First English Language Magazine Is Here*, The Atlantic (Jun. 30, 2010), http://www.theatlantic.com/international/archive/2010/06/al-qaedas-first-english-language-magazine-is-here/59006/ (discussing "Inspire," Al Qaeda's english language newspaper).

[74] *See* Joshua E. Keating, *Shots Fired - The Ten Worst Cyberattacks*, Foreign Policy (Feb. 27, 2012), http://www.foreignpolicy.com/articles/2012/02/24/shots_fired.

[75] Id.

[76] *See e.g.,* Clay Wilson, Cong. Research Serv., RL32114, Computer Attack and Cyberterrorism: Vulnerabilities and Policy Issues for Congress 5 (2005). (arguing that given the confluence of the United States' overwhelming military superirity, and its reliance on technology, future adversaries are likely to attempt acts of cyber-terrorism).

[77] Kevin Coleman, *The Increased Threat of Attacks on SCADA Systems*, Defense Tech, Sep. 26, 2011, http://defensetech.org/2011/09/26/the-increased-threat-of-attacks-on-scada-systems/ (reporting on the increased uses of SCADA control systems and the increasing numbers vulnerabilities found in those systems).

Hackers and foreign governments are increasingly able to launch sophisticated intrusions into the networks and systems that control critical civilian infrastructure. Given the integrated nature of cyberspace, computer-induced failures of power grids, transportation networks, or financial systems could cause massive physical damage and economic disruption. DoD operations—both at home and abroad—are dependent on this critical infrastructure.[78]

This quote hints at the existence of cyber-terrorism, but how exactly to define it?

Most definitions of cyber-terrorism are based on two general models: effects based criteria and intent-based criteria.[79] Many current definitions focus on one criterion to the exclusion or minimization of the other, with the result that the actions covered by the definition are either too broad or too narrow. This paper combines the effects and intent-based approaches, adding a requirement that the attacker be a non-state actor, arriving at the following definition for cyber-terrorism:

Premeditated, politically motivated computer network attacks perpetrated against noncombatant targets by subnational groups, designed to cause fear or anxiety in a civilian populace either by: a) inflicting, falsely appearing to inflict, or threatening to inflict, widespread damage to critical physical or informational infrastructure, national security related information systems, or critical economic systems; or b) causing, appearing to cause, or threatening to cause any type of severe physical damage or human casualties.

The elements and requirements contained in this definition, as well an explanation of the technical terms, will be discussed in the sub-sections below.

Overall, this definition intentionally mirrors the definition of terrorism utilized in Title 22, Chapter 38 of the U.S. Code, defining terrorism as "premeditated, politically motivated violence perpetrated against noncombatant targets by subnational groups or

---

[78] Dept. of Defense, Strategy for Operating in Cyberspace 4 (2011).
[79] *See* Clay Wilson, *Supra* note 76, at 4.

clandestine agents,"[80] in an attempt to maintain some consistency with a commonly used definition of terrorism in the U.S. Code. To that end, the element of "violence" in the definition of terrorism is replaced with a longer, more complicated list of effects. Although this makes the definition a bit more cumbersome, it was necessary to ensure both that the definition of cyber-terrorism did not become too broad as to include minor cyber-attacks, and to ensure that the unique ways in which cyber-attacks can affect a society were included. Should legislation that identifies critical infrastructure and economic systems, such as the Cybersecurity Act of 2012, be enacted into law those definitions and evaluations should be incorporated into this definition wherever possible. The remainder of this section will review the different terms and elements included in the above definition.

B. General Lexicon of Terms

The above-proposed definition included several terms that have developed into terms of art that should be identified. These terms build upon definitions in law or as used by government agencies.

1. Information System

An information system is any machine, network, or electronic device that contains stored information or is capable of processing data. This intentionally broad term covers hardware and software systems and the networks those systems operate on, typically referred to as "cyberspace." Hardware systems are primarily composed of computers, having the broad definition given in 18 U.S.C. §1030(e)(1):

---

[80] 22 U.S.C. § 2656f(d) (2006).

an electronic, magnetic, optical, electrochemical, or other high speed data

processing device performing logical, arithmetic, or storage functions, and

includes any data storage facility or communications facility directly related to or

operating in conjunction with such device, but such term does not include an

automated typewriter or typesetter, a portable hand held calculator, or other

similar device.

Cyberspace encompasses any type of network those hardware systems operate on, and is

defined by the DoD as the "global domain within the information environment consisting

of the interdependent network of information technology infrastructures, including the

Internet, telecommunications networks, computer systems, and embedded processors and

controllers."[81] Most often we think of the Internet as this network, as this is the network

most easily accessed by an outside party and the predominant network in the world today.

However, the object of a cyber-terrorist attack does not need to be on the Internet, or any

network at all, as seen with the Agent.btz attack, which used thumb drives to attack the

U.S. Government's classified networks.[82] Many critical infrastructure components are

intentionally not connected to the Internet as a security precaution, but remain vulnerable

to attack nevertheless.[83]

---

[81] DoD Dictionary, *Definition of Cyberspace,*
http://www.dtic.mil/doctrine/dod_dictionary/data/c/10160.html (last visited Feb. 4,
2012).

[82] *See, e.g.,* Kim Zetter, *The Return of the Worm That Ate the Pentagon,* WIRED (Dec. 9,
2011), http://www.wired.com/dangerroom/2011/12/worm-pentagon/ (describing a virus
that affected Department of Defense computers that spread through the use of thumb
drives).

[83] *See, e.g.,* Ellen Nakashima, *Cyber-intruder sparks massive federal response — and
debate over dealing with threats,* Wash. Post (Dec. 9, 2011),
http://www.washingtonpost.com/national/national-security/cyber-intruder-sparks-
response-debate/2011/12/06/gIQAxLuFgO_story.html (describing security precautions
that were meant to prevent infection of government classified computer systems and how
those measures were circumvented).

2. Computer Network Attack

Computer network attack (CNA) is a broad term used to mean any unauthorized access, or exceeding of one's access, to an information system that results in damage, enables potential future damage, or allows for future unauthorized access to information, on any information system. This is another intentionally broad term meant to cover the entire range of malicious activity that a perpetrator may take against an information system. The DoD defines CNA as "[a]ctions taken through the use of computer networks to disrupt, deny, degrade, or destroy information resident in computers and computer networks, or the computers and networks themselves."[84] The definition excludes using information systems to collect intelligence, which the DoD defines as "Computer Network Exploitation (CNE)."[85] However, this paper will include CNE with CNA to keep the meaning as broad as possible. CNA will be used for the remainder of this paper to refer to all types of cyber-attack.

3. Critical Infrastructure

Critical infrastructure is defined in law under the Critical Infrastructures Protection Act of 2001 as:

> systems and assets, physical or virtual, so vital to the United States that the incapacity or destruction of such systems and assets would have a debilitating impact on security, national economic security, national public health and safety, or any combination of those matters.[86]

---

[84] Dep't of Defense, Joint Publication 1-02, Dep't of Defense Dictionary of Military Terms 83 (2010).
[85] Id. at 65.
[86] 42 U.S.C. §5195c(e) (2006). *See generally* John D. Moteff, Cong. Research Serv., RL30153, Critical Infrastructures: Background, Policy, and Implementation.

Although an imprecise definition, examples of critical infrastructure generally include the power grid, telecommunication lines and towers, air traffic control, port controls, and primary repositories of economic data.[87]

The Senate Report accompanying the 1996 version of the Computer Fraud and Abuse Act (CFAA) recognized the potential for CNA on critical infrastructure:

> As the [National Information Infrastructure] and other network infrastructures continue to grow, computers will increasingly be used for access to critical services such as emergency response systems and air traffic control, and will be critical to other systems which we cannot yet anticipate.[88]

As government and private companies seek to become more efficient in the operations of critical infrastructure, these components become increasingly dependent on computer controls and networks for their operation.[89] The dependency on computer systems results in an increased vulnerability to CNA. Recently, the government, through the Department of Homeland Security has taken an increased role in protection of critical infrastructure information systems.[90]

---

[87] *See generally*, Dep't Homeland Sec., *Homeland Sec. Pres. Directive 7: Critical Infrastructure Identification, Prioritization, and Protection* (2003), available at http://www.dhs.gov/xabout/laws/gc_1214597989952.shtm#0.

[88] S. Rep. 104-357, at 11 (1996).

[89] *See,* J.A. Lewis, Center for Strategic & International Studies, *Assessing the risks of cyber terrorism, cyber war and other cyber threats* (Dec. 2002), *available at* http://csis.org/files/media/csis/pubs/021101_risks_of_cyberterror.pdf (arguing that attacks against critical infrastructure by cyber-weapons is primarily a business concern, and that the concern to national security is overstated).

[90] Janet Napolitano, Sec. of Homeland Security, *A Focused Effort on Cybersecurity*, Dep't of Homeland Security Leadership Journal (2009), http://journal.dhs.gov/2009/06/focused-effort-on-cybersecurity.html (describing DHS efforts in the area of cyber-security).

4. Terrorism

Generically, cyber-terrorism has been defined as the use of computers and the Internet to engage in terrorist activity.[91] Although this definition is simple and gets at the heart of cyber-terrorism, it also begs the question: what is terrorism? In the last half-century, terrorism has become a loaded term with significant legal and moral overtones. Congress has enacted several non-traditional laws, such as criminalizing material support to terrorism, that have pushed the boundaries of the Constitution.[92] Identifying a crime with terrorism generally brings extended sentences and has due process implications. Therefore, defining a crime that incorporates the term "terrorism" should be done carefully so as to not include lesser acts that are not on the same moral plane.

There are numerous definitions of terrorism in U.S. Code, this paper will examine some of the most commonly used. The U.S. Code includes the following definition in Title 22, Chapter 38: "[P]remeditated, politically motivated violence perpetrated against noncombatant targets by subnational groups or clandestine agents."[93] Title 18 of the U.S. Code (regarding criminal acts and criminal procedure) defines international terrorism as:

> [A]ctivities that . . . involve violent acts or acts dangerous to human life that are a violation of the criminal laws of the United States or of any State, or that would be a criminal violation if committed within the jurisdiction of the United States or

---

[91] *See, e.g.,* Clay Wilson, Cong. Research Serv., RL32114, Computer Attack and Cyberterrorism: Vulnerabilities and Policy Issues for Congress 5 (2005) (Wilson argues that defining any particular act as cyber-terrorism is problematic because of the inherent difficulties in determining the attackers identify, motive and intent, but recognizes the potential for cyber-terrorism).

[92] *See* Holder v. Humanitarian Law Project, 130 U.S. 2705 (2010) (holding that 18 U.S.C. § 2339B, Material Support to Designated Terrorist Organizations, did not violate the defendant's First Amendment rights when defendant provided the designated foreign terrorist organization training on peaceful dispute resolution).

[93] 22 U.S.C. § 2656f(d) (2006).

of any State; [and] appear to be intended . . . to intimidate or coerce a civilian

population; . . . to influence the policy of a government by intimidation or

coercion; or . . . to affect the conduct of a government by mass destruction,

assassination, or kidnapping; and [which] occur primarily outside the territorial

jurisdiction of the United States, or transcend national boundaries in terms of the

means by which they are accomplished, the persons they appear intended to

intimidate or coerce, or the locale in which their perpetrators operate or seek

asylum.[94]

The U.S. Code of Federal Regulations defines terrorism as "the unlawful use of

force and violence against persons or property to intimidate or coerce a government, the

civilian population, or any segment thereof, in furtherance of political or social

objectives."[95] Most definitions used by the United States include a variation on two

elements: 1) an act of violence; and 2) the attack must be political in nature, seeking to

influence governmental decisions; with some including requirements that the attack must

be aimed at civilians or non-belligerents, and/or be conducted by non-state actors.[96] As

will be discussed later, cyber-terrorism is distinct enough that terrorism need not be

precisely defined. However, the basic elements comprising most definitions of terrorism

in use by the United States should be understood. These elements are discussed below.

The first element, common to all definitions of terrorism, is that there be some act

that is violent in nature or dangerous to human life.[97] There is no specific formula to

determine what level of violence qualifies, but it is generally considered that the act be

---

[94] 18 U.S.C. § 2331(1) (2006).

[95] 28 C.F.R. § 0.85(l)

[96] *See e.g.*, Bruce Hoffman, Inside Terrorism 34 (2d ed., Colum. U. Press, 2006).

[97] Walter Laqueur, *The New Terrorism: Fanaticism and the Arms of Mass Destruction 6*
(Oxford University Press, 1999) (evaluating over a hundred definitions of terrorism and
finding the violence requirement is one universal element).

violent enough to intimidate the population at large, not just the subject of the attack.[98]

This intimidation, and the resulting fear or anxiety in that society, is at the heart of

terrorism. It is what creates the "terror." This distinction will be important later when

examining what type of CNA has enough effect on the population to be considered an act

of cyber-terrorism.

The second element typically required is that the attack be political in nature,

seeking to influence a government through violent actions.[99] Although there are other

crimes that are violent in nature, such as murder and mayhem, the political element

separates terrorism from crimes with similar results, such as murder.[100] Terrorist

organizations typically have defined motivations and stated end goals, such as the

Provisional Irish Republican Army, which desired to oust the British Government from

Northern Ireland,[101] or Al-Qaeda, which advocates for the withdrawal of western nations

from the middle-east and the establishment of a global Islamic caliphate.[102] The terrorist

creates "terror" through acts of large-scale violence, such as a bomb, chemical/biological

weapon, or other violent attack.[103] It is this fear and threat of further violence that is

---

[98] *See e.g.,* 18 U.S.C. § 2331(1) (2006).

[99] *See, e.g.,* 18 U.S.C. § 2331 (2006); *and* 50 U.S.C. § 1801(c)(2) (2006) (including a requirement the act intends (A) to intimidate or coerce a civilian population; (B) to influence the policy of a government by intimidation or coercion; or (C) to affect the conduct of a government by assassination or kidnapping).

[100] 18 U.S.C. § 1111 (2006) (defining murder generally as the unlawful killing of a human being with malice aforethought).

[101] *See generally* Ed Moloney, A Secret History of the IRA 246 (2003).

[102] *See* Christopher M. Blanchard, Cong. Research Serv., RL32759, *Al Qaeda: Statements and Evolving Ideology* (2007).

[103] *See generally* Steve Bowman, Cong. Research Serv., RL31332, Weapons of Mass Destruction: The Terrorist Threat (2002).

intended to motivate a government to change its policy toward the intended aim of the terrorist organization.[104]

The third element, which is less common in terrorism definitions, requires non-belligerents outside the scope of a military conflict to conduct the violence.[105] Violence aimed directly at military personnel by belligerents is generally not considered terrorism.[106] Examples of attacks on military outside the scope of a conflict include the 9/11 attack on the Pentagon[107] and the 1996 bombing of the Khobar Towers complex in Saudi Arabia.[108] Acts against the military within the scope of a conflict conducted by belligerents, are generally considered acts of warfare, even if they mimic terrorist attacks.[109] Cyber-attacks against military forces as part of a broader conflict is covered below under the category of armed attack in cyberspace. This is just one of the various categories of CNA that will be discussed in the next section.

---

[104] *See, e.g.*, Framing Terrorism: The News Media, the Government and the Public, 3,8 (Pippa Norris, Montague Kern, & Marion Just eds., 1 ed. 2003) (generally discussing news coverage of terrorism and how it frames public discussion of terrorism).

[105] *See* Jennifer Elsea, Cong. Research Serv., RL31191, Terrorism and the Law of War: Trying Terrorists as War Criminals before Military Commissions 14 (2002).

[106] *See e.g.,* 22 U.S.C. § 2656f(d)(2) (2006) (defining terrorism as "premeditated, politically motivated violence perpetrated against noncombatant targets by subnational groups or clandestine agents").

[107] Pentagon History - September 11, 2001, http://pentagon.osd.mil/september11.html (last visited Feb 21, 2012) (on Sept. 11, 2001, Al-Qaeda hijacked American Airlines flight 77 and flew it into the west side of the Pentagon, killing all aboard as well as over 100 people in the Pentagon).

[108] Rebecca Grant, *Death in the Desert,* Air Force, June 2006, at 48 (on June 25, 1996, a group of mostly Saudi nationals with ties to Iran and the Islamic Movement for Change exploded a car bomb outside the Air Force barracks in Dhahran, Saudi Arabia, killing 19 Airman).

[109] *See* Elsea, *supra* note 105, at 10-13.

C. Definitional Elements

This section will examine the elements contained in the proposed definition of cyber-terrorism and the reasons for their inclusion. Like the traditional elements of terrorism discussed above, cyber-terrorism should include an intent element, an effects element, and a requirement that the cyber-terrorist not be a non-state actor.

1. The Effects Element – Fear and Anxiety

The effects element of cyber-terrorism requires that the CNA cause fear or anxiety in a civilian populace through widespread damage to critical physical or informational infrastructure, national security related information systems, critical economic systems, or that result in severe physical damage or human casualties. This can occur through the actual causation of these effects, by causing the appearance or belief in these effects, or threatening to cause these effects, as they all have the potential to cause fear or anxiety in a populace. Some definitions of cyber-terrorism focus solely or predominantly on the effects of the act, subordinating the intent of the actor. For example, the informal, but commonly used, definition of cyber-terrorism as "hacking with a body count" is indicative of this approach.[110] The advantage of this definition is that the motivation of the attacker need not be determined. The CNA need only be evaluated on the basis on tangible outcomes, allowing a clear standard for determining when a CNA rises to the level of cyber-terrorism. If the result of the CNA is equivalent to the fear and anxiety caused by traditional terrorist actions, then it will be labeled an act of cyber-terrorism.

---

[110] Amara D. Angelica, *The New Face of War,* TechWeek.com (Nov. 2, 1998), http://www.transbay.net/~nessie/Pages/teds.html (quoting Barry Collin).

Focusing on the effects of a CNA also has the advantage of being able to distinguish between cyber-terrorists, who are a serious threat to national security, and online activists who conduct minor CNA to make points,[111] who are not serious threats. An online activist may seek to influence popular or government opinion by defacing a military or government website, but this does not make him a terrorist.[112] Some commonly used definitions of cyber-terrorism fail to make this distinction. For example, the Office of the Comptroller of the Currency defines cyber-terrorism as "[t]he use of computing resources against persons or property to intimidate or coerce a government, the civilian population, or any segment thereof, in furtherance of political or social objectives."[113] This definition contains no indication of how severe the CNA would have to be before it is defined as cyber-terrorism. Such an overbroad definition runs the risk of making cyber-terrorism such an overly broad term as to be inappropriately inclusive of misconduct not generally understood as terrorism.

Along with a tendency to be overbroad, the other problem with most effects elements in cyber-terrorism is they leave open the question of effects not traditionally associated with terrorist attacks, but that can have equally devastating effects on society. For example, a CNA could inflict great economic damage on a nation without inflicting civilian casualties by corrupting large amounts of economic data. Definitions of traditional terrorism typically incorporate an element of physical damage or civilian casualties, as these are historically the type of attacks that produce fear and anxiety in

---

[111] Such groups are commonly referred to as "hacktivists" and are discussed in greater detail below.

[112] *See* Michelle Delio, *Hacktivism and How It Got Here*, Wired (July 14, 2004), http://www.wired.com/techbiz/it/news/2004/07/64193.

[113] Office of the Comptroller of the Currency, Infrastructure Threats from Cyber-Terrorists 2 (Mar. 19, 1999).

society. However, to restrict cyber-terrorism to events where there are civilian casualties or large-scale physical destruction ignores a large range of highly malicious CNA. Therefore, physical damage or civilian casualties should not be the sole determinant in the effects element. It should also focus on the psychological effect the CNA has on the target society.

Under this paper's definition, the "effect" element requires a CNA that leads to either of the following: damage traditionally associated with terrorism, such as death, injury, water contamination, or release of radiological material; or damage uniquely caused by a CNA that could have an equivalent psychological impact on society, such as pipeline bursts, extended power outages, take-down of air-traffic control (ATC) systems or major loss of economic data.[114] However, the intended effects of CNA can often be hard to predict and distinguish, and the line between the two can be difficult to determine.[115] Therefore, it is necessary to also have an element of intent in a proper definition of cyber-terrorism.

2. The Intent Element - Motivation

The intent definition requires that CNA be premeditated and politically motivated. Similar to effects-based definitions, there are definitions currently in use that focus solely on the intent of the CNA, while ignoring its motivation. A typical intent-based definition of cyber-terrorism is that offered by Serge Krasavin, Ph.D., of the Computer Crime

---

[114] *See* Dorothy E. Denning, *Is Cyber Terror Next?*, Social Science Research Council, Nov. 1, 2001, http://essays.ssrc.org/sept11/essays/denning.htm (evaluating potential threats of cyber-terrorism in the immediate aftermath of 9/11).
[115] *See* Martin C. Libicki, *Cyberwar as a Confidence Game*, Strategie Studies Quarterly 132, 133 (Winter 2011).

Research Center. Dr. Krasavin defines cyber-terrorism as "use of information technology and means by terrorist groups and agents."[116]

This definition offers a much different approach by focusing on the actor, not the act. Accordingly, as long as a terrorist is using the information system towards his or her means, it does not matter what the result of that use is. Using e-mail to communicate with other terrorists would be an act of cyber-terrorism. However, the rapid spread of the Internet around the world means there likely is not a terrorist organization that does not use the Internet and computers for any number of reasons.[117] Thus, the category essentially becomes redundant to that of terrorism. This definition is an excellent description of "terrorist use of the Internet," but is not helpful in distinguishing cyber-terrorism from other type of CNA.

The advantage of an intent-based definition is it covers the full range of attacks both unique to CNA, such as damaging economic data, and similar to traditional terrorism, such as releasing poison gas. However, an attack for political motivations can run the entire spectrum of CNA, including basic denial of service attacks and government website defacement, to potentially major attacks, such as on SCADA controlled utilities. Intent-based definitions, like overly broad effects-based definitions, run the risk of making the category of cyber-terrorism so broad it becomes meaningless. We do not classify the graffiti artist who spray-paints "Out of Iraq" on a public wall as a terrorist partly because the term would lose its meaning. The same should hold for acts of cyber-terrorism.

---

[116] Serge Krasavin, Ph.D., *What is Cyber-terrorism?* Computer Crime Research Center, http://www.crime-research.org/library/Cyber-terrorism.htm (last visited Feb 7, 2012).
[117] See the following part for a discussion of terrorist use of the Internet.

The most useful approach is combining an element of motivation requiring the CNA be premeditated and politically motivated, with the above effects element. The term cyber-terrorism should recognize the purpose behind the attack: to undermine a government or motivate it to change its policies; and it should only recognize CNA with adequate effects: attacks that produce fear or anxiety in the populace. This combination will avoid the trap of being too narrow, allowing the inclusion of certain effects unique to CNA, while also avoiding being too broad - excluding those acts that are of a more trivial nature.

3. The Non-State Actor Requirement

Although not every definition includes a requirement that terrorist acts be conducted by non-state actors, most acts with effects similar to that of a terrorist act that are attributed directly to a state are considered acts of armed aggression. The reason is that such an attack is likely to be dealt with in a much different manner by governmental agencies, and would be viewed differently by the public. For example, if the intelligence operative of a foreign nation were to set off a bomb in the United States, and it was known that this operative was acting under the control of that foreign nation, it would be seen as an act of armed aggression by that state and dealt with as such. The same should be true for cyber-terrorism. However, the exclusion of this element is not fatal to the definition, and may be eliminated for certain applications.

One of the prime difficulties in cyber-terrorism will be deciding whether a state actor is responsible for the attack. Many experts believe that nations such as China and Russia, who have extensive CNA capabilities, use hacking groups not officially state related to mask state involvement in CNA against foreign powers. This is no new tactic in the world of terrorism, as we have seen with state-sponsors of terrorism such as Iran.[118]

However, the built-in anonymity of the Internet and the lack of physical infrastructure

required to launch an attack, make this tactic even more successful in cyberspace.

Whether a CNA is ultimately attributed to a state will depend upon the evidence

particular to the case, and the willingness of political leaders to place blame with state

actors. However, because the response options will be so entirely different against a state

actor, it is more useful to categorize those attacks as something other than cyber-

terrorism.

D. Current Definitions of Cyber-Terrorism

Having proposed a common working definition of cyber-terrorism, this section

analyzes the definitions that have either been offered by academics, or are in use by the

U.S. government. To start, the original definition came from Barry C. Collin, a senior

research fellow at the Institute for Security and Intelligence in California, in the 1980s.[119]

His vision of cyber-terrorism was one in which attacks conducted through computers

mirrored the effects of traditional acts of terrorism:[120]

> Like conventional terrorists, CyberTerrorists are out for blood. They try to do
> things like break into subway computer systems to cause a collision or use

---

[118] *See, e.g.*, Cent. Intelligence Agency, *The World Factbook - Iran*,
https://www.cia.gov/library/publications/the-world-factbook/geos/ir.html (last visited Feb
29, 2012) (describing Iran's designation as a state sponsor of terrorism for its activities in
Lebanon and elsewhere in the world).

[119] Barry C. Collin, The Future of CyberTerrorism: Where the Physical and virtual
Worlds Converge, 11th Annual International Symposium on Criminal Justice Issues, 15-
18 (March 1997) (as quoted by Dorothy E. Denning, *Activism, Hacktivism, and
Cyberterrorism: The Internet as a Tool for Influencing Foreign Policy* totse.com (2007),
http://www.totse2.com/totse/en/technology/cyberspace_the_new_frontier/cyberspc.html).

[120] Mohammad Iqbal, *Defining Cyberterrorism*, 22 J. Marshall J. Computer & Info. L.
397, 403 (2004) (quoting Barry Collin).

computers to tamper with power grids or food processing. However, unlike suicide bombers and roof-top snipers, CyberTerrorists attack from the comfort of home and can be in more than one place at a time through cyberspace. . . . CyberTerrorism can be far more damaging, and far more violent, than a 55-gallon drum of fuel and fertilizer. . . . CyberTerrorists' isolation from the results of their actions and the consequent lack of personal risk, make them particularly dangerous. . . . [T]he ease and low cost of CyberTerrorism combine to offer an attractive tool for once-conventional sociopaths.

Following this statement, there has bee no shortage of cyber-terrorism definitions offered. Many contain similar elements and themes, but the broad divergence in scope of these definitions signals the need for a definition that can be used as a common starting point. This section begins by looking at definitions used by the U.S. Government.

1. United States Government Definitions

Though not explicitly defined as cyber-terrorism, a form of it is contained in the U.S. Code. 18 U.S.C. §2332B(g)(5) (2006) defines the "federal crime of terrorism" and includes as predicate offenses two CFAA provisions, one relating to cyber-espionage and one related to computer damage.[121] If one of those two CFAA provisions is violated, and if that CFAA violation "is calculated to influence or affect the conduct of government by intimidation or coercion, or to retaliate against government conduct," then it meets this definition of terrorism.[122] The implications of this provision will be covered in greater depth later, but it is important to recognize that Congress has thought fit to include some CNA in one definition of terrorism under the U.S. Code.

---

[121] 18 U.S.C. § 1030(a)(1) (relating to cyber-espionage); and 18 U.S.C. § 1030(a)(5)(A) resulting in damage as defined in 18 U.S.C. § 1030(c)(4)(A)(i)(II) through (VI) (requiring damage to national security related computers or if the damage involves 10 or more computers).
[122] 18 U.S.C. § 2332B(g)(5) (2006).

Using the example in the opening section of this paper in which Anonymous attacked a FBI website in retaliation for its arrest of Kim Dotcom and others, Anonymous' actions meet the definition of the federal crime of terrorism. This definition meets the motivation element, as motivation is clearly covered in the federal crime of terrorism. However, it fails to sufficiently define the scope of the attack's effects. Under the predicate CFAA offenses, almost any denial of service attack against a national security website will fall under its definition. These denial of service attacks are serious and should be investigated, but they do not cause fear or anxiety in the populace. Despite this recognition of cyber-terrorism in the criminal code, most government agencies have developed their own definitions of cyber-terrorism. These definitions contain some important differences and an attempt should be made to make them more consistent.

The Federal Emergency Management Agency (FEMA) has defined cyber-terrorism as "unlawful attacks and threats of attack against computers, networks, and the information stored therein when done to intimidate or coerce a government or its people in furtherance of political or social objectives."[123] This definition incorporates an adequate intent element that appears in most definitions of terrorism and cyber-terrorism alike. It requires the attacker's objective to be political or social coercion against a government or it's people. The weakness of this definition again comes in the effects element, making no requirement as far as scale of attack goes. Under this definition, the lone wolf who hacks a web-page to post a political message, such as "Stop the War in Iraq," or temporarily takes down a DoJ public website to protest an arrest would be guilty

---

[123] Clay Wilson, Cong. Research Serv., RL32114, Botnets, Cybercrime, and Cyberterrorism: Vulnerabilities and Policy Issues for Congress 4 (2008) (quoting from the FEMA toolkit for terrorism responses).

of cyber-terrorism. Under this definition, the requirement that a CNA "intimidate or coerce" could be seen as requiring a more substantive attack, but it is too vague to be an effective definition.

The National Infrastructure Protection Center (NIPC) defines cyber terrorism as "a criminal act perpetrated through computers resulting in violence, death and/or destruction, and creating terror for the purpose of coercing a government to change its policies."[124] Unlike the previous definitions, which tended to be over-broad, this definition focuses more on the effects of a test, with the result that it is extremely narrow. The definition excludes all attacks not "resulting in violence, death and/or destruction," excluding some of the most devastating possibilities of CNA. An argument could be made that this definition is unnecessary as everything it states is already covered by definitions of terrorism. To be at its most useful, a definition of cyber-terrorism must include effects such as a takedown of economic systems or corruption of massive amounts of national security data, as this is where the unique capabilities of cyber-terrorism lie.

William L. Tafoya, Ph.D., writing in the FBI Law Enforcement Bulletin, defines cyber-terrorism as "the intimidation of civilian enterprise through the use of high technology to bring about political, religious, or ideological aims, actions that result in disabling or deleting critical infrastructure data or information."[125] Tafoya clarifies this definition through the example of wiping out the data of the Library of Congress, versus

---

[124] Clay Wilson, Cong. Research Serv., RL32114, Botnets, Cybercrime, and Cyberterrorism: Vulnerabilities and Policy Issues for Congress 4 (2003) (Quoting Ron Dick, then Director of the NIPC).

[125] William L. Tafoya, Ph.D., *Cyber Terror*, FBI Law Enforcement Bulletin, Nov. 2011, http://www.fbi.gov/stats-services/publications/law-enforcement-bulletin/november-2011/cyber-terror.

wiping out a single academic paper. The former would be seen as devastating and certainly affect people's quality of life, whereas the latter would have a limited effect on people's lives, outside that of the author.[126] This definition identifies "disabling or deleting critical infrastructure data or information" as the effect that would be required to meet the definition. This definition is the opposite of the FEMA definition, which required an element of violence. Instead, it does not account for physical harms at all, focusing solely on data. Recognizing this unique ability of CNA is important, but it need not be at the complete exclusion of all other types of harms. However, any definition of cyber-terrorism should similarly include attacks on critical data systems.

Any governmental definition of cyber-terrorism will need to be altered somewhat to fit with the goals of that agency, and this paper does not mean to suggest that all agencies use the proposed definition. But as has demonstrated above, the currently used definitions are so divergent as to make a common government-wide strategy to defeat cyber-terrorism more difficult. There should, at a minimum, be a consistency on the three basic elements, particularly the type of effects that are included. Consistency should also be sought with international organizations, and although not the focus of this paper, it is useful to see how one major member of the international community has defined cyber-terrorism.

2. United Nations Definition of Cyber-terrorism

The United Nations (UN) Counter-Terrorism Implementation Task Force (CTITF), although not explicitly using the term cyber-terrorism, recognizes that one of the ways a

---

[126] <u>Id.</u>

terrorist organization may use the Internet is the "[u]se of the Internet to perform terrorist attacks by remotely altering information on computer systems or disrupting the flow of data between computer systems."[127] The CTITF goes on to explain:[128]

> any cyber attack qualifying as 'terrorist' would ultimately still have to cause damage in the 'real world': for example, by interfering with a critical infrastructure system to the extent of causing loss of life or severe property damage. However, as dependence on online data and services increases, an attack that resulted only in widespread interruption of the Internet could, in future, cause sufficient devastation to qualify as a terrorist attack. However, categorizing such attacks as terrorist remains controversial. The damage resulting from such attacks, while potentially economically significant, to date their impact has been more on the level of a serious annoyance.

This definition, while a bit unwieldy, does an excellent job of recognizing that not only should violent attacks be included, but attacks on data may also serious enough to rise to the level of terrorism. This definition, however, fails to address the element of intent and the non-state actor requirement. As governments and world organizations have struggled with the definition and issue of cyber-terrorism, so have academics in the legal and security communities.

3. Academic Definitions

Most academic interest in large scale CNA tends to focus on cyber-warfare and the involvement of state actors. This is logical given the greater size and resources of

---

[127] U.N. Counter-Terrorism Implementation Task Force, *Report of the Working Group on Countering the Use of the Internet for Terrorist Purposes* 8 (February 2009), http://www.un.org/terrorism/pdfs/wg6-internet_rev1.pdf.
[128] Id. at 9.

governments such as China, Russia, and the United States. Some prominent cyber-security experts, however, have focused on cyber-terrorism: the possibility of large scale CNA by non-state actors. One of the earliest, and most widely cited academic descriptions of cyber-terrorism comes from security expert Dorothy Denning:[129]

> Cyberterrorism is the convergence of terrorism and cyberspace. It is generally understood to mean unlawful attacks and threats of attack against computers, networks, and the information stored therein when done to intimidate or coerce a government or its people in furtherance of political or social objectives. Further, to qualify as cyberterrorism, an attack should result in violence against persons or property, or at least cause enough harm to generate fear. Attacks that lead to death or bodily injury, explosions, plane crashes, water contamination, or severe economic loss would be examples. Serious attacks against critical infrastructures could be acts of cyberterrorism, depending on their impact. Attacks that disrupt nonessential services or that are mainly a costly nuisance would not.

Although it primarily focuses on violent acts, Denning's description does include attacks that cause severe economic loss. She excludes attacks that are minor in nature, steering the definition towards more significant attacks. Non-violent types of attacks may also be covered by the phrase "or at least cause enough harm to generate fear,"[130] but it is difficult to draw clear guidelines from this statement. It also declines to state whether the

---

[129] Dorothy E. Denning, *Cyberterrorism: Testimony before the Special Oversight Panel on Terrorism, H. Comm. on the Armed Services* (May 23, 2000), http://www.cs.georgetown.edu/~denning/infosec/cyberterror.html (arguing that a definition of cyber-terrorism should involve a component of violence or harming of critical infrastructure, and that, at the time, it was mostly theoretical but could arise in the future).
[130] Id.

attacker must be a non-state actor. Overall, however, it is an excellent foundation from
which to formulate a precise definition that meets the criteria of being broad enough to
include unique CNA, such as attacks on data only, and narrow enough to exclude monor
activist attacks.

The Center for Strategic and International Studies (CSIS) defined cyber-terrorism
as "the use of computer network tools to shut down critical national infrastructures (such
as energy, transportation, government operations) or to coerce or intimidate a government
or civilian population."[131] This definition is at once both precise: "shut down critical
national infrastructures," and vague: "coerce or intimidate government or civilian
populace." It fails to define what level of coercion or intimidation is required before it
goes from being a protest, to an act of terrorism. Although it suggests a higher level of
attack by explicitly including critical infrastructure, it fails to be more precise beyond that
particular category.

Kelly Gable provided a similar definition, including "efforts by terrorists to use the
Internet to hijack computer systems, bring down the international financial system, or
commit analogous terrorist actions in cyberspace."[132] Gable focuses on the international
finance system, as opposed to critical infrastructure, but also includes "analogous terrorist
actions," which clearly suggests violent acts. This definition is useful in identifying the
need to include CNA causing drastic effects on the financial system in any definition.

---

[131] J.A. Lewis, *Assessing the risks of cyber terrorism, cyber war and other cyber threats*,
Center for Strategic & International Studies (Dec. 2002),
http://csis.org/files/media/csis/pubs/021101_risks_of_cyberterror.pdf.
[132] Kelly A. Gable, *Cyber-Apocalypse Now: Securing the Internet Against
Cyberterrorism and Using Universal Jurisdiction as a Deterrent*, 43 Vand. J. Transnat'l
L. 57, 62 (2010).

Susan Brenner, another noted cyber-security expert, posits a basic definition of cyber-terrorism, stating: "[g]enerically, cyberterrorism consists of using computer technology to engage in terrorist activity."[133] Recognizing the broad nature of this definition, Brenner goes on to further define it in several important ways. Brenner excludes from cyber-terrorism attacks that originate through the Internet, but have the end result of large scale destruction, what she terms as a "Weapon of Mass Destruction" attack.[134] She provides the example of hacking into the controls of a nuclear power plant and causing a Chernobyl style meltdown.[135] Although it seems counter-intuitive to exclude this action from cyber-terrorism, Brenner argues that such an attack would primarily be remembered as a nuclear terrorist attack, not a cyber-attack, and therefore should not be considered cyber-terrorism.[136] Brenner argues that we do not define a car bomb attack as automotive-terrorism, so why define a cyber-attack as cyber-terrorism?[137] It should also be noted that Brenner did not see this type of attack as a real possibility, but rather a conceptual problem only.[138]

Whereas Brenner makes a good point that CNA producing violence is a "terrorist" attack in the traditional sense, there is still good reason to further classify it as a cyber-terrorist attack, particularly if the definition is to be used as a common working definition

---

[133] Susan W. Brenner, *"At Light Speed" - Attribution and Response to Cybercrime/Terrorism/Warfare*, 97 J. Crim. L. & Criminology 397, 386 (2007) (categorizing cyber-threats and focusing on attribution as the key element to be solved in battling those threats).
[134] <u>Id.</u> at 390-391.
[135] <u>Id.</u>
[136] <u>Id.</u>
[137] <u>Id.</u> at 391.
[138] <u>Id.</u>

for government agencies. First, a separate classification is needed to gear policy makers and law enforcement towards appropriate methods of prevention and response.

Prevention of a traditional terrorist attack on a nuclear plant is vastly different from a CNA, and will require different thought processes, security measures, and, as this paper later argues, changes to the law. Traditional attack prevention involves protection of physical security on the grounds surrounding of the plant, while CNA prevention involves protection of the plant's information systems. Similarly, a law enforcement investigation of a traditional terrorist attack would require vastly different techniques and expertise than a CNA on that same plant. Staying with the automotive analogy, law enforcement would use substantially the same techniques to investigate a physical bombing of a power station whether the bomber used a vehicle or a suicide vest to attack the station. However, the same could not be said if the attack was conducted through information systems.

The second category of cyber-terrorism that Brenner proposes is a "Weapon of Mass Distraction."[139] This would be a CNA not with violent, physical effects, but psychological effects that could undermine the faith in government.[140] Brenner provides the example of leading people to believe, through a hacked news website, that there was a suitcase nuclear device on a city bus, leading to mass panic and possibly death.[141] Certainly, this is a more realistic scenario than the attack on the nuclear plant, given the lower level of sophistication required. As previously noted, Lulz was able to place a news

---

[139] Id. at 391-3.
[140] Id.
[141] Id. at 392.

story on PBS that Tupac Shakur was still alive several years after his actual death.[142] Additionally, this type of attack could be accomplished completely through the Internet, unlike CNA against a nuclear plant, which would probably requiring introducing the attack from the inside.[143]

Because of the lower level of sophistication required, Brenner views this type of attack as more than a theoretical possibility. As more and more news is relayed through Internet news outlets, Facebook, Twitter, instant messaging and other Internet based sources, the potential panic that would likely result from a "weapons of mass distraction" attack is high. Causing the appearance of a terrorist attack through CNA represents a major threat that should be accounted for in any definition of of cyber-terrorism.

Brenner's final cyber-terrorism category is a "Weapon of Mass Disruption."[144] This type of attack utilizes CNA against infrastructure components such as an electrical grid or gas supply.[145] The cyber-terrorist's goal would be to undermine the populace's faith in government by interrupting essential services.[146] Brenner sees this as a more realistic possibility than that which produces violent, catastrophic effects.[147] These types of attacks have been attempted with limited success, though they have yet to cause

---

[142] *See* Kevin Poulsen, *Hacktivists Scorch PBS in Retaliation for WikiLeaks Documentary,* WIRED (May 30, 2011), http://www.wired.com/threatlevel/2011/05/lulzsec/.
[143] *See* Nuclear Energy Institute - Plant Security, http://www.nei.org/keyissues/safetyandsecurity/plantsecurity/ (last visited Feb 29, 2012) (describing nuclear plant operations as isolated from the Internet and other networks).
[144] Brenner, *"At Light Speed," supra* note 133, at 393-5.
[145] Id.
[146] Id.
[147] Id.

widespread fear or panic.[148] However, this type of attack seems different more in terms of scale than type from the "Weapon of Mass Destruction" category. If a hacker could alter the gas supply to shut it down, certainly that same hacker could overload the gas supply and possibly cause an explosion.

Overall, Brenner's point was that cyber-terrorism should not be treated on the level of war, for the greatest potential harms were either too theoretical or simply straight terrorism, but should instead be treated as crime.[149] However, following Al-Qaeda's attacks on 9/11, terrorist attacks have become a category unto themselves and the response has included participation by the intelligence agencies, law enforcement, and the military. The threats posed by terrorism have prompted the passage of new laws and the development of new law enforcement techniques. If it is possible a cyber-terrorist attack could seriously undermine a citizenry's faith in government, as Brenner suggests it could, then policy makers should identify cyber-terrorism as unique from cyber-crime, and devote serious attention to prevention and response.

E. Categories of Computer Network Attack

If cyber-terrorism is to be recognized as a unique type of CNA, it is important to examine those other types of CNA to understand how they are distinguished. Within the category of CNA are several sub-categories, which this paper will distinguish by using three factors: damage done to the target information system, motivation of the attack, and

---

[148] Tony Smith, *Hacker jailed for revenge sewage attacks*, The Register (Oct. 31, 2001), http://www.theregister.co.uk/2001/10/31/hacker_jailed_for_revenge_sewage/.

[149] Brenner, *"At Light Speed," supra* note 133, at 398-399.

identity of the attacker. By identifying each of the three factors in a particular attack, the attack can be categorized and response options determined.

1. Cyber-crime

This paper defines a cyber-crime as any level of CNA, conducted by any party, for any purpose considered illegal under domestic or international law. This category is the broadest category of CNA, and includes every type of CNA outside those in an armed conflict that do not violate the laws of war. Under U.S. domestic law, it is essentially any action that violates the CFAA.

Cyber-crimes need not have the information system as a target, as the definition includes those attacks simply using the information system as a tool. A current definition in use by the Computer Crime Research Center defines cyber-crime as "crimes committed on the Internet using the computer as either a tool or a targeted victim."[150] Although this paper argues a CNA does not have to be conducted through the Internet, this definition accurately reflects that information systems can be used to effectuate an attack, not just serve as the target. CNAs frequently use other means of accessing information systems than the Internet. The Stuxnet virus, for example, is thought to have been placed onto information systems using an infected removable drive, given that the target system was not connected to the Internet.[151] This is important for a discussion of

---

[150] Aghatise E. Joseph, *Cybercrime Definition*, Computer Crime Research Center (June 28, 2006), http://www.crime-research.org/articles/joseph06/.

[151] *See* William J. Broad, John Markoff & David E. Sanger, *Stuxnet Worm Used Against Iran Was Tested in Israel*, N. Y. Times (Jan. 15, 2011), http://www.nytimes.com/2011/01/16/world/middleeast/16stuxnet.html; *see also* Zetter, *supra* note 82.

cyber-terrorism as many critical infrastructure components are not connected to outside networks as a security measure, and must be accessed through another means.

2. Cyber-espionage

Cyber-espionage is a CNA by a state actor for the motivation of collecting intelligence against another state, or a government contractor of that state dealing in national security, which causes minimal damage or disruption to the information system. This definition does not incorporate non-national security related corporate espionage, as that is a more traditional cyber-crime. This is not to say that corporate espionage does not have national security implications. According to the DoD:[152]

> Every year, an amount of intellectual property larger than that contained in the Library of Congress is stolen from networks maintained by U.S. businesses, universities, and government departments and agencies. As military strength ultimately depends on economic vitality, sustained intellectual property losses erode both U.S. military effectiveness and national competitiveness in the global economy.

However, the tools for dealing with traditional criminal actions such as corporate espionage diverge sharply from counter-intelligence.

Cyber-espionage also does not incorporate a CNA by a state actor that causes more than minor damage or degradation to a foreign network, which I would classify as an armed attack in cyberspace. Whether or not an armed attack in cyberspace rises to the level of an act of war is a complicated calculus that has received much analysis from

---

[152] Dept. of Defense, Strategy for Operating in Cyberspace 4 (2011).

government sources and academics alike. However, armed attack in cyberspace is generally not considered an acceptable practice.[153] Cyber-espionage, on the other hand, is generally considered acceptable internationally as a form of espionage, and it is rapidly rising as a major national security concern.[154] That international law neither clearly condones nor explicitly proscribes the conduct tends to support the conclusion that "[e]spionage is nothing but the violation of someone else's laws."[155] States do criminalize spying under domestic laws, applying it to any individual spies they catch,[156] but for cyber-espionage, of course, the chances of apprehension are remote, since states can conduct it without putting their agents physically inside a foreign nation.

One of the best examples of cyber-espionage was the cyber-espionage ring known as "Titan Rain."[157] Discovered in 2003, websites in China targeted unclassified networks in the DoD and other federal agencies.[158] The attacks were eventually traced to the province of Guangdong, China, but never definitively traced to the Chinese

---

[153] Even though many experts suspect that the Russian government engages in CNA, they continually refuse to acknowledge any direct involvement. *See e.g., Estonia hit by "Moscow cyber war,"* BBC (May 17, 2007), http://news.bbc.co.uk/2/hi/europe/6665145.stm.

[154] *See Chinese step up computer espionage against United States,* N.Y. Times, (Oct. 20, 2008), http://www.nytimes.com/2008/11/20/world/americas/20iht-spy.4.18006075.html?scp=1&sq=chinese%20computer%20espionage&st=cse (reporting on a Congressional committee looking into the dramatic rise in online theft of sensitive information by China).

[155] U.S. Intelligence Agencies and Activities: Risks and Control of Foreign Intelligence, Part 5: Hearing Before the H. Select Comm. on Intelligence, 94th Cong. 1767 (1975) (statement of Mitchell Rogovin, Special Counsel to the Director of Central Intelligence).

[156] *See e.g.,* 18 U.S.C. § 792 et seq (2006).

[157] Joshua E. Keating, *Shots Fired - The Ten Worst Cyberattacks*, Foreign Policy (Feb. 27, 2012), http://www.foreignpolicy.com/articles/2012/02/24/shots_fired (describing Titan Rain as one of the ten worst cyber-attacks).

[158] Bradley Graham, *Hackers Attack Via Chinese Web Sites,* Wash. Post (Aug. 25, 2005), http://www.washingtonpost.com/wp-dyn/content/article/2005/08/24/AR2005082402318.html.

government.[159] Included in the information stolen by the cyber-spies were schematics for

NASA's Mars Reconnaissance Orbiter, a huge collection of files from Redstone Arsenal,

home to the Army Aviation and Missile Command, and Falconview 3.2, the flight-

planning software used by the Army and Air Force.[160] Alan Paller, the director of the

SANS Institute, an education and research organization focusing on cyber-security, stated

that, based upon the techniques used, the cyber-spies were working for the Chinese

military.[161] These attacks, however, were not aimed at disrupting the operation of United

States government networks, simply obtaining information from them. Had they

disrupted the networks to a large degree, they would be properly categorized as an armed

attack in cyberspace.

3. Armed Attack in Cyberspace

Armed attack in cyberspace is a CNA by a state actor, or a non-state actor under the

direction of a state actor, that causes more than minor destruction, damage, or

degradation to an information system itself, or anything outside the information system

that is destroyed, damaged, or degraded as a result of the CNA through the use of an

information system. This term is often equated with cyber-warfare, defined by Susan

Brenner as follows:[162]

---

[159] *See* Nathan Thornburgh, *The Invasion of the Chinese Cyberspies*, Time (Aug. 29, 2005), http://www.time.com/time/printout/0,8816,1098961,00.html (reporting on a civilian, Shawn Carpenter, who was able to track the spies to Guangdong while working as an computer security analyst for Sandia National Laboratories).

[160] Id.

[161] *Hacker attacks in US linked to Chinese military*, Breitbart (Dec. 12, 2005), http://www.breitbart.com/article.php?id=051212224756.jwmkvntb&show_article=1.

[162] Susan W. Brenner, *"At Light Speed" - Attribution and Response to Cybercrime/Terrorism/Warfare*, 97 J. Crim. L. & Criminology 397, 401 (2007).

Cyberwarfare is the conduct of military operations by virtual means. It consists of nation-states' using cyberspace to achieve the same ends that they pursue through the use of conventional military force: achieving advantages over a competing nation-state or preventing a competing nation-state from achieving advantages over them.

This close alliance with warfare has led many to question what kind of CNA would rise to the level of "use of force" and trigger law of war considerations.[163] The DoD provides a vague standard, stating that "[a]s in the physical world, a determination of what is a 'threat or use of force' in cyberspace must be made in the context in which the activity occurs, and it involves an analysis by the affected states of the effect and purpose of the actions in question."[164] Charles Dunlap, former Deputy Staff Judge Advocate of the Air Force and current visiting professor of law at Duke University, argues that CNA resulting in violent effects is equivalent to armed attacks and constitutes a use of force.[165] Additionally, according to Dunlap, when there is a use of force, the Laws of War should apply and govern the conduct of state actors just as in traditional warfare.[166] However, rarely have states acknowledged any role in cyber-warfare outside of actions taken during

---

[163] *See generally* Charles J. Dunlap Jr., *Perspectives for Cyber Strategists on Law for Cyberwar*, 5 Strategic Studies Quarterly 81-99 (2011), *available at:* http://scholarship.law.duke.edu/faculty_scholarship/2368 (arguing that the laws comprising the Law of Armed Conflict as existing are adequate to deal with the new development of cyber-warfare).

[164] Dept. of Defense, *Cyberspace Policy Report: A Report to Congress Pursuant to the National Defense Authorization Act for Fiscal Year 2011, Section 934* 9 (Nov. 2011). http://www.defense.gov/home/features/2011/0411_cyberstrategy/docs/NDAA%20Sectio n%20934%20Report_For%20webpage.pdf.

[165] Siobhan Gorman & Julian E. Barnes, *Cyber Combat: Act of War*, Wall St. J. (May 31, 2011), http://online.wsj.com/article/SB10001424052702304563104576355623135782718.html.

[166] Id.

a declared conflict.[167] Most actions that are taken by governments are more precisely

defined as covert actions. A classic example of a covert action in cyberspace is the

infiltration of the Stuxnet computer virus against Iran; assuming that, as most analysts

suspect, it was launched by a nation state.[168] This paper will identify all such cyber-

attacks as armed attacks in cyberspace.

A good example of armed attack in cyberspace is the 2008 conflict between Russia

and Georgia.[169] The conflict was over a province of Georgia, South Ossetia, which sought

independence from Georgia.[170] The Russian government backed the separatists and on

August 8, 2008, the two sides clashed militarily.[171] The Georgians were pushed out of

South Ossetia on August 10 after two days of fighting the Russian army.[172] Just as the

military conflict was taking place, a shadow conflict was also taking place on the

Internet. According to Georgian officials, Russian state-sponsored hackers launched an

extensive CNA campaign against Georgian government websites.[173] Georgian President

Mikheil Saakashvili's website, the website of the Ministry of Foreign Affairs, and that of

the Ministry of Defense were all forced offline as part of the attack.[174]

---

[167] *See* Richard A. Clarke & Robert Knake, Cyber War: The Next Threat to National Security and What to Do About It 69 (Reprint ed. 2011) (describing the use of armed attack in cyberspace by the United States Air Force in the Iraq War).

[168] *See* Broad, Markoff & Sanger, *supra* note 151.

[169] Peter Finn, *A Two-Sided Descent Into Full-Scale War*, Wash. Post (Aug. 17, 2008), http://www.washingtonpost.com/wp-dyn/content/article/2008/08/16/AR2008081600502_pf.html.

[170] Id.

[171] Id.

[172] Id.

[173] Asher Moses, *Georgian Websites Forced Offline in "cyber War,"* Sydney Morning Herald (Aug. 12, 2008), http://www.smh.com.au/news/technology/georgian-websites-forced-offline-in-cyber-war/2008/08/12/1218306848654.html.

[174] Id.

This CNA was unique in that it occurred in conjunction with a larger military campaign. Although it did not appear to affect the military operations, it did suppress the Georgian government's ability to spread information to both its people and those abroad.[175] It is likely a harbinger of future military conflicts in which cyber-warfare will have an increasingly large role to play. But what if these attacks had occurred completely outside a military conflict and were conducted by civilians? How should they be categorized in that situation? The answer would likely be as "hacktivists."

4. Hacktivism

Hacktivists are often mixed in with cyber-terrorism, given that the difference between the two is in some ways only a matter of degree. The term was coined by a group of hackers called the Cult of the Dead Cow, who wanted to use computer hacking to foster human rights and free expression.[176] These groups are non-state actors who conduct CNA with political motivations.[177] The level of these attacks, however, are relatively minor and do not cause effects traditionally associated with terrorism, such as: fear or panic in the civilian populace, affect national security, or damage critical infrastructure, to include economic data.[178] Although these groups do commit crimes, hacktivist groups are primarily distinguished from most cyber-criminals through their

---

[175] Id.

[176] *See* Michelle Delio, *Hacktivism and How It Got Here*, Wired (July 14, 2004), http://www.wired.com/techbiz/it/news/2004/07/64193.

[177] U.S. Gov't Accountability Office, Statement for the record to the Subcommittee on Terrorism and Homeland Security, Sen., Cybersecurity: Continued efforts are needed to protect information systems from evolving threats 4 (2009), available at http:// www.defense.gov/home/features/2010/0410_cybersec/docs/d10230t.pdf [hereinafter *GAO cyber-security statement for the record*].

[178] *See generally* Karson K. Thompson, *Not Like an Egyptian: Cybersecurity and the Internet Kill Switch Debate*, 90 Tex L. Rev. 465, 476 (2011) (defining and providing examples of hacktivism).

motivations.[179] They are motivated by a desired to change a policy, practice or mode of thinking, as opposed to monetary gain or other traditional criminal motivation.[180] Hacktivists have participated in numerous CNA opposing (or favoring) various groups or causes, such as attacks on Visa and MasterCard,[181] and supporting WikiLeaks.[182] Hacktivism is certainly a growing phenomenon,[183] but, given the limited nature of the attacks as defined, probably not a major threat to national security.[184] If the damage caused by hacktivists were to substantially increase and pose a threat to national security, however, they would rise to the level of cyber-terrorism.

One of the largest hacktivist operations seen to date was termed the "50 days of Lulz."[185] In 2011 a group of hackers going by the name of Lulz, or Lulzsec, underwent a concentrated number of CNA focused on political causes.[186] For example, PBS' popular news show Frontline aired a show on Wikileaks that Lulz disagreed with in May 2011.[187] In response, Lulz hacked into the PBS website and posted a fake news story about Tupac

---

[179] Id.

[180] *See GAO cyber-security statement for the record, supra* note 177, at 4.

[181] *Wikileaks "data war" gathers pace*, BBC (Dec. 9, 2010), http://www.bbc.co.uk/news/technology-11935539 (Visa and MasterCard were hit with denial of service attacks after they withdrew their services from Wikileaks).

[182] Peter Ludlow, *WikiLeaks and Hacktivist Culture*, The Nation (Sept. 15, 2010), http://www.thenation.com/article/154780/wikileaks-and-hacktivist-culture (discussing the prominence of WIkileaks in the hacktivist sub-culture).

[183] John P. Mello, Jr., Hacktivism Trumps Money as Motivation for Denial-of-Service Attacks, PCWorld, February 7, 2012, http://www.pcworld.com/article/249442/hacktivism_trumps_money_as_motivation_for_denialofservice_attacks.html (stating that hacktivism is the most widespread motivation for Distributed Denial of Service attacks on the Internet).

[184] *See* Lewis, *supra* note 131.

[185] *See* Keating, *supra* note 157.

[186] Id.

[187] *See* Poulsen, *supra* note 142.

Shakur being alive and living in New Zealand.[188] Lulz also posted e-mail addresses and

passwords for over 200 of PBS affiliate stations around the country.[189] The group also

took down the Central Intelligence Agency's website and released the personal

information of millions of Play Station Network's users.[190] At least one leader of this

group, known as Topiary, was arrested in the Shetland Islands for his hacking in

connection with Lulz.[191] The CNA by Lulz was certainly serious, particularly the release

of personal data for the PlayStation Network users. However, it is a stretch to argue that

the release of personal data, in the age of Facebook, rises to the level of terrorism. Just as

definitions of terrorism require that the effects of the act rise to a certain level, so should

a definition of cyber-terrorism be careful to ensure these acts of "hacktivism" are not

included.

5. Terrorist Use of the Internet

When most people think of terrorists and the Internet, they do not think of taking

down the electric grid through a cyber-attack, they think of Al-Qaeda posting a video

online or using the Internet to promote their message.[192] The presence of terrorist

organizations on the Internet has thus far been dominated by terrorist organizations

utilizing the Internet for planning, coordination, propaganda, and recruitment – what I

---

[188] Id.

[189] Id.

[190] *See* Keating, *supra* note 157.

[191] Josh Halliday, Charles Arthur & James Ball, *LulzSec hacking suspect "Topiary" arrested*, the Guardian (July 27, 2011),
http://www.guardian.co.uk/technology/2011/jul/27/lulzsec-hacking-suspect-topiary-arrested.

[192] *See* Eben Kaplan, *Terrorists and the Internet,* Council on Foreign Relations (Jan. 8, 2009), http://www.cfr.org/terrorism-and-technology/terrorists-internet/p10005 (Discussing the advantages of the Internet to terrorist organizations and they currently use it).

will define as "terrorist use of the Internet."[193] One of the earliest terrorist organizations

to realize the potential of the Internet was Al-Qaeda,[194] and it became one of its most

effective tools in becoming an international terrorist organization.[195] As terrorist

organizations utilize the Internet's anonymity and flexibility, it "erodes the ability of our

security services to hit them when they're most vulnerable, when they're moving," said

Michael Scheuer, former chief of the CIA unit that tracked Osama bin Laden.[196] In a

similar thought, longtime State Department expert Dennis Pluchinsky finds the global

jihad movement has become a "Web-directed" phenomenon.[197]

Cyberspace is an ideal platform to communicate and coordinate activities. Its speed,

simplicity, ease of access, and anonymity makes it difficult to monitor and control.[198]

There are also reports that terrorist organizations have turned to traditional cyber-crimes

such as theft and fraud to raise funds.[199] Some experts believe that without a state

---

[193] *See* Gabriel Weimann, Terror on the Internet: The New Arena, the New Challenges (1 ed. 2006) (A study of how modern terrorist organizations exploit the Internet to raise funds, recruit members, plan and launch attacks, and publicize their results). *See also,* Benjamin R. Davis, *Ending the Cyber Jihad: Combating Terrorist Exploitation of the Internet with the Rule of Law and Improved Tools for Cyber Governance,* 15 CommLaw Conspectus 119 (2006) (arguing that the U.S. and foreign governments, as well as international bodies like ICANN, have failed to adequately respond to the use of the Internet by terrorist organizations).

[194] N.Y. Times, *Al Qaeda* (Jan. 31, 2012), http://topics.nytimes.com/top/reference/timestopics/organizations/a/al_qaeda/index.html?scp=1&sq=al-qaeda%20internet&st=cse (last visited Feb 5, 2012).

[195] Steve Coll & Susan B. Glasser, *Terrorists Turn to the Web as Base of Operations,* Wash. Post (Aug. 7, 2005), http://www.washingtonpost.com/wp-dyn/content/article/2005/08/05/AR2005080501138.html (charting Al Qaeda's migration from operating primarily in real space to operating in cyberspace).

[196] Id.

[197] Id.

[198] *See* Weimann, *supra* note 193, at 25.

[199] Jon Swartz, *Terrorists' use of Internet spreads,* USA Today, Feb. 21, 2005, http://www.usatoday.com/money/industries/technology/2005-02-20-cyber-terror-

sponsor, or an influx of highly trained computer personnel, this is as far as they will go.[200]

Others, including the FBI, believe Al-Qaeda may try some act of cyber-terrorism.[201]

Either way, international terrorist organizations have learned the power of the Internet

and are willing to use it in creative ways to accomplish their objectives. However, using

information systems to further one's organization is distinctly different from using those

information systems as a weapon of terror. Al-Qaeda does not need to write malicious

code or manipulate SCADA systems to help organize and fund the organizations, or

spread propaganda. The two categories will certainly connect in some ways, but the tools

needed to counter them are fundamentally different.

Having defined cyber-terrorism, examined the elements of that definition, and

distinguished it from other types of CNA, the next part of this paper will examine

examples of major CNA to determine whether those attacks would be appropriately

categorized as cyber-terrorism.

---

usat_x.htm (Citing examples of terrorists organizations using fraud on the internet to finance their operations).

[200] Mark Ward, *Cyber terrorism "overhyped,"* BBC, Mar. 14, 2003, http://news.bbc.co.uk/2/hi/technology/2850541.stm (Stating the belief of several security experts that would-be online terrorists lack the technical expertise and resources to engage in cyber-terrorism).

[201] Cybersecurity: Preventing Terrorist Attacks and Protecting Privacy in Cyberspace: Hearing Before the Subcomm. on Terrorism and Homeland Sec. of the S. Judiciary Comm., 111th Cong. 2 (Statement of Steven R. Chabinsky, Dep. Asst. Dir., Cyber Division, FBI).

Part III. Recent Examples of Computer Network Attack

"CIA TANGO DOWN" - 10 February 2012 Tweet by the hacker group Anonymous

This section examines several recent major examples of CNA to determine if they should be classified as cyber-terrorism. Specifically, this section examines the effects, motives, and targets of the examples of CNA, measuring them against the elements set out in the definition of cyber-terrorism.

A. Anonymous

Anonymous is an affiliation of hackers who have conducted an increasingly large number of attacks since their beginnings around 2003.[202] They are thought to be associated with Lulz, discussed in part II.[203] Some of their most notable targets include private organizations such as the Church of Scientology[204] and Sony,[205] as well as government organizations from the CIA,[206] to the governments of Tunisia[207] and Iran.[208]

---

[202] Chris Landers, *Serious Business: Anonymous Takes On Scientology (and Doesn't Afraid of Anything)*, Baltimore City Paper (Apr. 2, 2008), http://www2.citypaper.com/columns/story.asp?id=15543 (describing a 2008 dispute between the Church of Scientology and the hacking group Anonymous that was a response in part to the Church of Scientology's claims of online copyright infringement).
[203] *See* Poulsen, *supra* note 142.
[204] Id.
[205] Elinor Millis, *Sony sites offline after Anonymous attack threats, CNET*, Apr. 6, 2011 4:52 PM, http://news.cnet.com/8301-27080_3-20051482-245.html (after Sony filed suit against individuals who had "jailbroken" software for its popular gaming system, Anonymous launched denial of service attacks against several sites associated with Sony).
[206] Nicole Perlroth, *Anonymous Says It Knocked C.I.A. Site Offline*, N.Y. Times Bits Blog, Feb. 10, 2012, http://bits.blogs.nytimes.com/2012/02/10/anonymous-says-it-knocked-c-i-a-site-offline/ (the attack against the CIA website followed closely after the

Although many of their attacks have shown a high degree of coordination, the nature of the organization is somewhat informal.[209] In a 2011 interview with IT World reporter Dan Tynan, one of the leaders of Anonymous, known as Commander X, stated there were approximately ten thousand members of Anonymous worldwide.[210] Commander X stated that their targets are selected by looking at several factors, including: 1) whether there are already protests in place against the target; 2) if the protests are non-violent; 3) they have a likelihood of success; and 4) there is a clear moral imperative.[211] Commander X does not define whose "moral imperative" guides their actions.

Clearly, Anonymous sees its actions as civil disobedience, using the language of morality to justify its actions. An example of this moralistic language was the recent launch of a cyber-campaign against Israel. On February 11, 2012, a video purportedly released by Anonymous promised a "crusade" against Israel.[212] The stated aim of

---

FBI arrests of the owners of a popular music downloading site, Megaupload.com, but it was unclear if the arrests were related to the attacks on the CIA sites).

[207] Max Read, *Anonymous Attacks Tunisian Government over Wikileaks Censorship*, Gawker (Jan. 3, 2011), http://gawker.com/5723104/anonymous-attacks-tunisian-government-over-wikileaks-censorship (in December 2010, the government of Tunisia reportedly blocked its country's Internet users from accessing Wikileaks, or any news outlet that reported on the leaked cables regarding Tunisia, prompting denial of service attacks by Anonymous on the Tunisian government's websites).

[208] Kevin Fogarty, *"Anonymous" attacks Iran, calls for volunteers to help U.S. tornado victims*, IT World, May 2, 2011, http://www.itworld.com/security/161241/anonymous-attacks-iran-calls-volunteers-help-us-tornado-victims.

[209] Dan Tynan, *A conversation with Commander X*, IT World, Feb. 18, 2011, http://www.itworld.com/internet/137590/conversation-commander-x.

[210] Id.

[211] Id.

[212] Given the nature of Anonymous announcements, it would be easy for anyone to claim action in their name. However, this author could find no statement repudiating the intent launch a CNA against Israel by Anonymous.

Anonymous was "systematically removing [Israel] from the internet."[213] The video cited Israel's "Zionest bigotry" and population displacement as reasons for the promised attacks.[214]

Looking at these attacks, in conjunction with the attack outlined at the beginning of this paper, it raises the question: Is Anonymous a "hacktivist" organization, or are they cyber-terrorists? As already detailed, their attacks against justice and national security websites such as the FBI and DoJ, as well as the CIA attack, meet the definition of a federal crime of terrorism. But should the simple act of temporarily taking down a government website result in labeling a group as "terrorists?"

Looking at the elements presented in this paper's definition of cyber-terrorism, the answer becomes clearer. First is the question of intent, which Anonymous clearly meets. The goal of Anonymous is to undermine groups and organizations they do not agree with, including governments.[215] They also meet the requirement of being a non-state group, as they contain no identified ties to a state. So the last question is whether the effects of their attacks are designed to cause fear or anxiety in a civilian populace through effects that cause widespread damage to critical physical or informational infrastructure, national security related information systems, critical economic systems, or that result in severe physical damage or human casualties.

---

[213] Donald MacIntyre, *Hacking group threatens 'crusade' against Israel*, The Independent, Feb. 11, 2012.
[214] Id.
[215] Tynan, *supra* note 209. Commander X stated that their goal when dealing with foreign "dictators" is to remove them from power.

None of the attacks conducted by Anonymous or its affiliates have directly caused physical damage or human casualties,[216] but they have affected operation of web operations for some national security related agencies through denial of service attacks. However, CNA resulting in the temporary takedown of websites, such as those of the FBI, White House, or CIA, should not be considered widespread damage. The public sites of these agencies, while important, are generally media outlets and for general notices to the public.[217] Additionally, the hacked websites are typically only down for a brief period of time.[218] Should these attacks occur during a public emergency with increased reliance on those sites for vital information, however, the effects would likely meet the definitional element of cyber-terrorism.

Anonymous has also gone so far as to eavesdrop on the phone calls between the FBI and Scotland Yard.[219] In this CNA, Anonymous was able to listen in on a conference call discussing efforts against hacking groups, raising the question of how deeply the group had infiltrated various law enforcement agencies.[220] This infiltration should be considered more severe than the taking down of a website, as it could affect operations and, potentially, national security. However, the public effects of such actions are limited

---

[216] *See* Elinor Millis, *Keeping up with the hackers (chart)*, CNET (Feb. 8, 2012), http://news.cnet.com/8301-27080_3-20071830-245/keeping-up-with-the-hackers-chart/.

[217] *See e.g.,* CIA Website, https://www.cia.gov/, last accessed 12 Feb. 2012.

[218] *See, e.g.,* Christopher Williams, *Anonymous attacks FBI website over Megaupload raids*, The Telegraph (Jan. 20, 2012), http://www.telegraph.co.uk/technology/news/9027246/Anonymous-attacks-FBI-website-over-Megaupload-raids.html (describing the Anonymous attacks on the FBI website and stating that the site was only don for a brief period of time, although the sites for the Motion Picture Association of America were down considerably longer).

[219] Leo Kelion, *Hackers breach FBI-UK police call, BBC* (Feb. 3, 2012), http://www.bbc.co.uk/news/world-us-canada-16875921.

[220] Id.

and should not be considered cyber-terrorism. Anonymous has not limited itself to denial of service attacks and other types of CNA may be a bit different.

In August 2011, the Bay Area Rapid Transit (BART) administration in San Francisco announced that they would cut cell phone service in tunnels as a response to protests over the shooting of a man by BART police.[221] Following this announcement, Anonymous leaked the names, phone numbers and passwords of BART riders.[222] Although Anonymous apologized to the riders for the release of their information, they blamed the release on BART for having lax security practices.[223] The city of Oakland police chief responded by calling the CNA an act of cyber-terrorism.[224] Loss of privacy data can be of great concern to Americans, and certainly affected these individuals lives more than a website disruption, but does it rise to the level of fear and anxiety?

As personal information placed on information systems becomes more prevalent, it also becomes more vulnerable to theft. An entire generation has become comfortable putting large amounts of personal information on the Internet through Facebook, Twitter and other social media outlets. Although most people trust that this data is somewhat secure, an entire industry has grown up around information security and identity

---

[221] David Streitfeld, *Bay Area Officials Cut Cell Coverage to Thwart Protestors*, N.Y. Times Bits Blog (Aug. 12, 2011), http://bits.blogs.nytimes.com/2011/08/12/bay-area-authorities-cut-cell-coverage-to-thwart-protestors/.
[222] Joshua Brustein, *Anonymous to BART: We Hack. We Organize, Too*, N.Y. Times Bits Blog (Aug. 15, 2011), http://bits.blogs.nytimes.com/2011/08/15/anonymous-to-bart-we-hack-we-organize-too/.
[223] Id.
[224] Matthew Artz, *Oakland officials condemn release of personal information by Anonymous*, San Jose Mercury News (Feb. 7, 2012), http://www.mercurynews.com/occupy/ci_19910127.

protection with companies such as Lifelock, Debix, and TrustedID.[225] There seems to be

a constant flow of news stories about government agencies, banks, and other companies

losing the privacy data of their clients or constituents.[226] Has the knowledge that so much

of our personal data is now in the hands of third parties limited the effect of a release

such as that of Anonymous? The line is a difficult one to draw, but in this case, with the

data limited to user names and passwords, the loss is not substantial enough that it should

be considered cyber-terrorism.

Thus, the actions of Anonymous, while troublesome to many,[227] do not yet rise to

the level of cyber-terrorism. Their rhetoric may suggest radical or even occasionally

violent aims, but their actions do not rise to that level.[228] However, this does not mean

that as their capabilities increase they will not attempt CNA that rises to the level of

cyber-terrorism. The National Security Agency (NSA) has warned that by 2014,

Anonymous could have the ability to bring down portions of the U.S. Power grid, which

---

[225] *See* Bruce Schneier, *The Pros and Cons of LifeLock*, WIRED (June 12, 2008), http://www.wired.com/politics/security/commentary/securitymatters/2008/06/securitymatters_0612?currentPage=all.

[226] *See generally* Mark Sullivan, *Protect Our Data! A Digital Consumer Bill of Rights*, PCWorld, Feb. 9, 2012, http://www.pcworld.com/article/249558/protect_our_data_a_digital_consumer_bill_of_rights.html.

[227] *See, e.g.,* Steven Musil, *Interpol sweep nets 25 Anonymous suspects*, CNET (Feb. 28, 2012), http://news.cnet.com/8301-1009_3-57387203-83/interpol-sweep-nets-25-anonymous-suspects/ (reporting that Interpol has arrested 25 members of Anonymous across Europe and South America in response to coordinated attacks by the group on websites in Colombia and Chile).

[228] *See* Tynan, supra note 209, (in the interview with Commander X, in response to questions about Wikileaks founder Julian Assange, stated: "[i]f they harm one hair upon Julian Assange's head, or if they destroy or damage WikiLeaks - the PLF WILL bring down the wrath of f***ing god on them").

should be considered cyber-terrorism as a CNA on critical infrastructure.[229] NSA had

been silent regarding Anonymous to this point, making the statement particularly

notable.[230] Additionally, Anonymous announced plans to "blackout" the Internet by

attacking the Domain Name System to protest "our irresponsible leaders and the beloved

bankers who are starving the world for their own selfish needs out of sheer sadistic

fun."[231] Time will tell if Anonymous truly has the intention and capability to carry out

such attacks. Given the nature of the organizations and the manner in which they

distribute their messages, it is difficult to determine whether these statements are

legitimately from Anonymous. At some point in the future, however, they may meet the

definition of a cyber-terrorist organization.

---

[229] Siobhan Gorman, *Alert on Hacker Power Play,* Wall St. J. (Feb. 21, 2012),
http://online.wsj.com/article/SB10001424052970204059804577229390105521090.html?
mod=WSJ_hp_MIDDLENexttoWhatsNewsThird (Gen. Keith Alexander, director of the
NSA, reportedly issued the warning in meetings with the White House and lawmakers);
see also Elizabeth Flock, *Anonymous attacks WSJ page hours after story warning group
is getting more powerful,* Wash. Post (Feb. 22, 2012),
http://www.washingtonpost.com/blogs/blogpost/post/anonymous-attacks-wsj-page-hours-
after-story-warning-group-is-getting-more-
powerful/2012/02/22/gIQA7QlFTR_blog.html?tid=sm_twitter_washingtonpost (after the
Wall Street Journal reported on Gen. Alexander's comments regarding Anonymous,
several Wall Street Journal Facebook pages were attacked by a German faction of
Anonymous).
[230] Kevin Fogarty, *NSA: Anonymous may take down U.S. power grid in two years*, IT
World (Feb. 21, 2012), http://www.itworld.com/security/251904/nsa-anonymous-may-
take-down-us-power-grid-two-years (stating that the NSA has neither considered
Anonymous a major threat to national security, nor ignored their capabilities).
[231] Jeremy Kirk, *Anonymous threatens to DDOS root Internet servers*, IT World (Feb. 20,
2012), http://www.itworld.com/security/251450/anonymous-threatens-ddos-root-internet-
servers (Anonymous announced it would launch an action on March 31, 2012 as part of
"Operation Global Blackout" that would target the root Domain Name System (DNS)
servers, however, experts state they are not likely to be successful).

B. ILOVEYOU virus

Anonymous is an example of a hacktivist group that has generally well-defined motivations, but whose attacks to this point are considered more of nuisance than a true threat to national security.[232] Opposite this, are a variety of attacks that have resulted in damage on a larger scale, but with less defined motivations. The ILOVEYOU virus and variants are a prime example of this type of CNA. The ILOVEYOU virus was estimated to have hit 45 million users and cost billions of dollars in damage.[233] The suspected attacker, Onel de Guzman, was apparently motivated by his thesis on computer vulnerabilities being rejected.[234] Given a political motivation, a physical bombing in the United States, even if no injuries occurred, causing billions in damages, would likely meet the definition of an act of terrorism.[235] However, a different analysis must be used in examining CNA. The effects of CNA are generally much more widespread and lack the pure shock of a physical attack. Therefore, the working definition of cyber-terrorism should be analyzed to determine whether an act of cyber-terrorism has truly taken place.

Examining this paper's definition of cyber-terrorism, the ILOVEYOU virus fails to rise to the level of cyber-terrorism. First, there is insufficient evidence that the motivation

---

[232] *See e.g.,* David Goldman, *Hacker group Anonymous is a nuisance, not a threat,* CNNMoney (Jan. 20, 2012), http://money.cnn.com/2012/01/20/technology/anonymous_hack/index.htm (calling Anonymous the "graffiti artists of the Internet").

[233] *I love you Virus,* Oracle ThinkQuest Education Foundation, http://library.thinkquest.org/04oct/00460/ILoveYou.html, last accessed 14 February 2012.

[234] Mark Landler, *A Filipino Linked to "Love Bug" Talks About His License to Hack,* N.Y. Times (Oct. 21, 2000), http://www.nytimes.com/2000/10/21/business/a-filipino-linked-to-love-bug-talks-about-his-license-to-hack.html?src=pm (Mr. Guzman reportedly submitted a thesis proposal on stealing passwords to gain free access to the Internet, which was rejected prompting him to drop out of school).

[235] *See* part II(B)(4) for U.S. Code definitions of terrorism.

of the attack was political.[236] The attacks did not appear to target government or national

security institutions.[237] Additionally, no message was released in conjunction with the

attack declaring an intent to undermine governments or influence policy.[238] Examining

the effects element, the answer is less clear. Although the attack was not aimed at national

security systems or infrastructure, it did have a significant effect on business[239] and

affected the networks of the CIA, Pentagon, and British Parliament.[240] Given the scale of

the damage, had these attacks been politically motivated, they would likely have risen to

the level of cyber-terrorism. However, failing the intent element, the ILOVEYOU should

be categorized generally as a cyber-crime.

C. US Power Grid

In April 2009, U.S. officials discovered hackers from Russia, China and other

countries had gained access to the U.S. power grid and left behind tools that could have

destroyed system controls.[241] The intrusions could not be definitively traced to either

---

[236] *See* Landler, supra note 234.

[237] Id.

[238] Id.

[239] Id.

[240] John Markoff, *April 30-May 6; An "I Love You" Virus Becomes Anything But*, N.Y. Times (May 7, 2000), http://www.nytimes.com/2000/05/07/weekinreview/april-30-may-6-an-i-love-you-virus-becomes-anything-but.html (reporting that the White House, the Pentagon, Congress and the British House of Commons were among those affected by the ILOVEYOU virus).

[241] Siobhan Gorman, *Electricity Grid in U.S. Penetrated By Spies,* Wall St. J., Apr. 8, 2009, http://online.wsj.com/article/SB123914805204099085.html (Reporting on the discovered intrusions into the information systems controlling portions of the U.S. power grid and the calls for the implementation of increased security measures); *see also* James A. Lewis, *The Electrical Grid as a Target for Cyber Attack,* Center for Strategic and International Studies, March 2010, *available at* http://csis.org/files/publication/100322_ElectricalGridAsATargetforCyberAttack.pdf (evaluating the risks of CNA on components of the electrical grid system).

state or non-state actors.[242] Nor were the motivations of the intrusions clearly understood, as the attacks were never actually carried out.[243] Speculations include a belief that Russian and Chinese governments gained access so that, in the event of a future conflict, the grid could be shut down or otherwise affected.[244]

The threat to the various power grids operating in the United States has prompted the Energy Department to launch an initiative into protecting the grid from CNA.[245] Losing control over the power grid could have cascading effects with disastrous consequences for hospitals, emergency responders, defense and law enforcement agencies, and the financial sector, among others.[246] In an armed conflict, the power grid is often among the first wave targets because of its ability to debilitate a nation's command and control structure.[247] Given the potential effect on society, a CNA that takes down a significant portion of a region's power grid for any extended period of time passes the effects test of a cyber-terrorism event. If the 2009 intrusions were the result of a non-state actor, then it should be considered an act in preparation for a cyber-terrorist attack, and treated just as seriously as an attempted attack.

---

[242] Id.

[243] Id.

[244] Id.

[245] Stephen Lawton, *Energy Department to analyze power grid cyber threats*, SC Magazine (Jan. 9, 2012), http://www.scmagazine.com/energy-department-to-analyze-power-grid-cyber-threats/article/222399/ (reporting on the Electric Sector Cybersecurity Risk Management Maturity project, a federal program headed by the Department of Energy to find and contain gaps in the cyber security defenses protecting the nation's electric grid).

[246] Lewis, *supra* note 241, at 1.

[247] *See* Thomas E. Griffith, Jr., *Strategic Attack of National Electrical Systems,* Air Power and Maneuver Warfare, Oct. 1994, available at http://www.comw.org/pda/fulltext/griffith.pdf (describing the history and purpose behind military attacks on electrical infrastructure).

D. Stuxnet

Between June 2009 and May 2010, a type of virus known as a worm,[248] was

discovered to have damaged Siemens supervisory control and data acquisition (SCADA)

systems that controlled centrifuges that were part of the Iranian nuclear program.[249] The

worm most likely infected the software through the use of a portable drive, such as a

thumb drive.[250] Given the sophistication of the CNA, experts conclude it would have

required the resources of a national government to engineer it, and the most likely culprit

was Israel.[251] Stuxnet initially spread indiscriminately, but the virus it contained was

designed to target only a very specific type of system, and therefore would not affect

targets other than those intended.[252] Although there are no reports of radiation leakage

from the effected sites, the NATO ambassador to Russia stated the virus "could lead to a

new Chernobyl."[253]

The Stuxnet virus should not be considered an act of cyber-terrorism because the

prevailing opinion is that it was a covert CNA conducted by a nation state.[254] Therefore, it

is appropriately categorized as an armed attack in cyberspace. However, it is interesting

---

[248] A worm is a type of CNA that replicates itself and sends those copies to other systems it comes in contact with. Worms can carry other computer viruses, or simply replicate and spread to use up bandwidth.

[249] John Markoff, *Stuxnet Software Worm Hit 5 Industrial Facilities in Iran*, N.Y. Times (Feb. 11, 2011), http://www.nytimes.com/2011/02/13/science/13stuxnet.html.

[250] Id.

[251] *See* William J. Broad, John Markoff & David E. Sanger, *Stuxnet Worm Used Against Iran Was Tested in Israel*, N.Y. Times (Jan. 15, 2011), http://www.nytimes.com/2011/01/16/world/middleeast/16stuxnet.html (some experts point to a secret facility in Israel's Negev desert where they claim Israel has a set of nuclear centrifuges similar to Iran's, where they tested Stuxnet).

[252] Jonathen Fildes, *"Nuclear virus" targets uncovered*, BBC (Feb. 15, 2011), http://www.bbc.co.uk/news/technology-12465688.

[253] Id.

[254] *See* Broad, Markoff & Sanger, *supra* note 251.

from a cyber-terrorism perspective because it represents the potential for future cyber-terrorist attacks on SCADA software operating critical infrastructure systems. That no deaths or violence resulted from the Stuxnet virus is not a factor weighing against classification as cyber-terrorism. Knowing that a nuclear facility has been targeted would be enough to cause a state of fear for those living near an affected facility. Were it to be revealed that this CNA was actually the result of a non-state actor, it should certainly be considered cyber-terrorism.

Under almost any definition of terrorism, an attack on a nuclear facility for political purposes would rank as a terrorist attack.[255] Given the potentially severe consequences of CNA on nuclear facilities, or similar facilities such as chemical plants producing dangerous gases, these types of attacks should receive particularly close attention. A step in the direction of treating sophisticated cyber-weapons with unique potential for cyber-terrorism, such as Stuxnet, would be to classify these weapons as Weapons of Mass Destruction. I will discuss how this should be done in the final part of this paper.

E. Estonia

In April of 2007, Estonia, a former Soviet satellite state with a large ethic Russian minority, was one of the most wired nations in the world.[256] The Estonians had pioneered a system of "e-government," making many government services and functions available

---

[255] *See e.g.,* 18 U.S.C. § 2332B(g)(5)(i) (2006) (listing offenses against nuclear materials among the predicate offenses for the federal crime of terrorism).

[256] Ian Traynor, *Russia accused of unleashing cyberwar to disable Estonia*, the Guardian, May 17, 2007, http://www.guardian.co.uk/world/2007/may/17/topstories3.russia.

through the Internet.[257] Estonia prided itself on both its Internet savvy and cyber-security.[258]

This was the backdrop when on April 27, 2007, the government of Estonia moved a Soviet-era Russian war memorial from a central square in the capital Talinn to another location, prompting massive protests from the ethnic Russian minority in Estonia and outrage from Russians abroad.[259] In conjunction with the physical protests, a three-week wave of CNA was launched against Estonia, primarily attacking the websites of Estonia's "e-government,"[260] dramatically reducing the government's ability to function. Combinations of different types of cyber-weapons were inflicted upon national Internet services.[261] Included were denial of service attacks shutting down much of the e-government services and hacking into government and media websites to alter their content.[262] Additionally, most of Estonia's media outlets were taken down by denial of service attacks, preventing reporting on what was happening in Estonia.[263] The damage as a result was estimated to be in the tens of millions of Euros.[264]

The CNA against Estonia may be the closest case of pure cyber-terrorism yet seen. The attacks were politically motivated and affected Estonia in a unique way. Estonian society was tied more deeply into the Internet than probably any other nation at the time.

---

[257] Clark Boyd, *Estonia opens politics to the web*, BBC (May 7, 2004), http://news.bbc.co.uk/2/hi/technology/3690661.stm (following independence from the Soviet Union, Estonia made a nationwide push to educate citizens in use of the Internet and place as many government functions online as possible).

[258] Traynor, *supra* note 256.

[259] Id.

[260] Id.

[261] Id.

[262] Id.

[263] Id.

[264] Ian Traynor, *Web attackers used a million computers, says Estonia*, the Guardian (May 17, 2007), http://www.guardian.co.uk/technology/2007/may/18/news.russia.

Estonia was also prepared to fend off a major CNA better than any country. Estonia has

pride in their network security and held a feeling of invulnerability to large scale CNA.

Although their security prevented the attack from being worse, their feeling of

invulnerability was shattered.[265]

The three weeks of CNA Estonia endured was difficult for their citizens, but the

psychological effect on the citizenry is difficult to read. Mikhel Tammet, the chair of

Estonia's cyber-defense co-ordination committee, believed the attack to be an act of

terrorism, stating:

> This is a kind of terrorism, the act of terrorism is not to steal from a state, or even
>
> to conquer it. It is, as the word suggests, to sow terror itself. If a highly IT country
>
> cannot carry out its every day activities, like banking, it sows terror among the
>
> people.[266]

Tammet's use of the word terrorism may have been intended to pressure Russia into

investigating the attacks, but it may also have reflected the anxiety of the nation as a

whole, given the unique connection, through the Internet, of the government and people

of Estonia.[267] Thus it meets the effects test not necessarily due to the nature of the attacks,

but because of the nature of their society.

---

[265] *See* Cyrus Farivar, *Cyberwar I,* Slate (May 22, 2007),
http://www.slate.com/articles/technology/technology/2007/05/cyberwar_i.html
(Reporting on the lessons learned from the CNA on Estonia).
[266] Adrian Blomfield, *Estonia calls for Nato cyber-terrorism strategy,* The Telegraph
(May 18, 2007), http://www.telegraph.co.uk/news/worldnews/1551963/Estonia-calls-for-
Nato-cyber-terrorism-strategy.html.
[267] *Estonia hit by "Moscow cyber war,"* BBC (May 17, 2007),
http://news.bbc.co.uk/2/hi/europe/6665145.stm.

The last remaining question in examining the CNA against Estonia is who conducted the attacks. Determining whether the attackers were the Russian government or just angry Russian civilians was never completely answered and represents the difficulty of determining attribution even in large-scale attacks.[268] Jaak Aaviksoo, Estonia's defense minister, stated "[t]here is not sufficient evidence of a [Russian] governmental role."[269] Estonia estimated at least one million computers were used in the attack. However, this many computers can be controlled were relatively ease by a hacker using a bot-net.[270] Estonia did discover that many of the attacks were routed through Russian government servers, but again, this was inconclusive.[271] The ambiguity of who conducted the CNA against Estonia is an excellent example of the difficulty attribution creates in classifying a CNA.

---

[268] Ian Traynor, *Web attackers used a million computers, says Estonia, supra* note 264; *but see* Robert Coalson, *Behind The Estonia Cyberattacks,* Radio Free Europe (Mar. 6, 2009), http://www.rferl.org/content/Behind_The_Estonia_Cyberattacks/1505613.html (describing an remark by a State Duma Deputy from the pro-Kremlin Unified Russia party that his assistant was responsible for coordinating the attack, but clarifying that his assistant acted on his own).

[269] Id.

[270] Id.

[271] Id.

Part IV. The Current Law and Problems

"The pessimist sees difficulty in every opportunity. The optimist sees the opportunity in

every difficulty." - Winston Churchill

In the previous sections this paper sought to define cyber-terrorism and place it in

the context of some recent examples of CNA. The next question is logically what to do

about it? To answer that question, this part first examines the main hindrance in

combating CNA in general, and cyber-terrorism specifically: attribution. It then examines

current domestic cyber-crime and counter-terror laws to determine how these existing

laws might be used to counter cyber-terrorism.

A. The Dilemma of Attribution

Perhaps the greatest challenge in confronting cyber-terrorism is the problem of

attribution: identifying the party or parties responsible for a CNA.[272] The problem of

attribution in the context of the Internet is, in large part, inherent in the structure of the

system.[273] Many hackers are now able to "spoof" Internet Protocol Addresses, allowing

---

[272] *See* Gregory N. Larsen & David A. Wheeler, *Techniques For Cyber Attack Attribution,* Inst. For Def. Analyses, 1-2 (2003) (describing technological barriers to correct attribution of cyber-attacks); *and* Stephen Dycus, Congress's Role in Cyber Warfare, 4 J. Nat'l Security L. & Pol'y 155, 163 (stating that the attribution problem effectively eliminates traditional deterrence and response options).

[273] *See* Larsen & Wheeler, supra note 272, at 2-4; and Dycus, *supra* note 272.

their CNA to appear to originate from another location.[274] This is an issue common to all cyber-crimes and well recognized by government and private industry alike. The DoD states that:[275] "[t]he Internet was designed to be collaborative, rapidly expandable, and easily adaptable to technological innovation. Information flow took precedence over content integrity; identity authentication was less important than connectivity." President Barack Obama stated that "[t]he speed and anonymity of cyber attacks makes distinguishing among the actions of terrorists, criminals, and nation states difficult."[276] The anonymity enabled by the Internet has proved remarkably adept at foiling law enforcement attempts at enforcing laws governing and deterring cyber-crime.

Without the ability to catch and prosecute, there is little deterrence for would be cyber-criminals.[277] For this reason, many jurisdictions place harsher penalties on cyber-crimes, in relation to similar crimes conducted without the use of information systems.[278] As the current head of U.S. Cyber Command, then Lieutenant General Keith Alexander, put it: "The bottom line is, the only way to deter cyber attack is to work to catch perpetrators and take strong and public action when we do."[279] Attribution is a necessity

---

[274] Kelly A. Gable, *Cyber-Apocalypse Now: Securing the Internet Against Cyberterrorism and Using Universal Jurisdiction as a Deterrent*, 43 Vand. J. Transnat'l L. 57, 102 (2010).

[275] Dept. of Defense, Strategy for Operating in Cyberspace 2 (2011).

[276] The White House, The National Strategy to Secure Cyberspace 19, 64 (2003).

[277] *See* Kathryn Stephens, *A Review of the Cybersecurity Legislative Proposal*, National Security Cyberspace Institute, 1 (2011) (reviewing 2011 U.S. government cyber-security initiatives).

[278] Id.

[279] Advance Questions for Lt. Gen. Keith Alexander, USA Nominee for Commander, U.S. Cyber Command Before the S. Armed Serv. Comm., 111th Cong. 23 (2010), available at http://armed-services.senate.gov/statemnt/2010/04%20April/Alexander%2004-15-10.pdf.

to enable traditional deterrence as well as distinguishing between the categories of CNA.[280]

Susan Brenner framed the issue of attribution elegantly, stating: "[c]yberspace fractures the crime scene into shards."[281] One shard is the place, or places, where the attack is felt. In widespread attacks such as the ILOVEYOU virus, there may be millions of shards worldwide.[282] Additional shards include the information systems through which the attack was conducted.[283] Expert cyber-criminals tend to route their attack through a maze of servers across the world to maintain anonymity.[284] Finally, there are the shards of the attackers, who may have planned and launched the attack from multiple information systems at multiple locations across the globe.[285] And as is the case of some Distributed Denial of Service attacks, the attacking computers may be operating without their owner having any idea of the attack.[286]

This shattering of the crime scene can complicate efforts to track the perpetrators immensely. Whereas most traditional crimes require some physical proximity between attacker and victim, the same is not true in cyberspace. Law enforcement agents are forced to navigate a web of state, federal, and international jurisdictions to trace an attack

---

[280] *See* Derek E. Bambauer, *Conundrum*, 96 Minn. L. Rev. 584, 598 (2011) (arguing that information, not systems should be the focus of cyber-security); and Susan W. Brenner, *"At Light Speed" - Attribution and Response to Cybercrime/Terrorism/Warfare*, 97 J. Crim. L. & Criminology 397, 438 (2007).

[281] Brenner, *"At Light Speed," supra* note 280, at 418.

[282] *I love you Virus*, Oracle ThinkQuest Education Foundation, http://library.thinkquest.org/04oct/00460/ILoveYou.html, last accessed 14 February 2012.

[283] Brenner, *"At Light Speed," supra* note 280, at 418-9.

[284] Id.

[285] Id.

[286] *See e.g.,* Franz Stefan-Grady, *Africa's Cyber WMD*, Foreign Policy, Mar. 24, 2010, http://www.foreignpolicy.com/articles/2010/03/24/africas_cyber_wmd.

to its origin, and then must tie an individual or individuals to a information system from which the attack was launched.[287] A serious result of this fracturing is the problem of false positives, where investigators believe that an intermediary point of transmission to be the originating point for the attack.[288]

Discussion on how to deal with the attribution dilemma has led to many interesting ideas, including utilizing civilian enforcement to help deter cyber-criminals.[289] For attacks on a greater scale, some have favored imputing attribution directly to the state where the attack originated, under a strict liability theory.[290] This is an approach some have also suggested for traditional acts of terrorism.[291] The difficulty in applying this theory to CNA is ease of launching an attack from any state in the world. Would it be just to hold Senegal responsible if an Iranian cyber-terrorist traveled to Dakar, connected to the Internet, and launched his attack that had been planned and developed in Tehran? This theory also assumes that governments around the world have the financial or technical capabilities to adequately monitor their networks.

---

[287] *See generally* Darrel Menthe, *Jurisdiction In Cyberspace: A Theory of International Spaces* 4 Mich. Telecomm. & Tech. L. Rev. 69 (1998), available at http://www.mttlr.org/volfour/menthe.html (examining jurisdictional laws and arguing Internet jurisdiction should be analogized to Antarctica, outer space, and the high seas, and treated as an "international space").

[288] Brenner, *"At Light Speed," supra* note 280, at 418.

[289] *See e.g.,* Brenner, "At Light Speed," *supra* note 280, at 465-74 (advocating a redistribution of responsibility for the identification of cyber criminals to civilians to improve cybercrime investigations).

[290] David E. Graham, *Cyber Threats and the Law of War*, 4 J. Nat'l Sec. L. & Pol'y 87, 92-93 (2010) (seeking to impute responsibility to states for attacks originating from that state's territory); *see also* Matthew J. Sklerov, *Solving the Dilemma of State Responses to Cyberattacks: A Justification for the Use of Active Defenses Against States Who Neglect Their Duty to Prevent*, 201 Mil. L. Rev. 1 (2009) (arguing that states use against cyber-defenses against CNA emanating from states that do not adequately prevent such attacks).

[291] Vincent-Joël Proulx, *Babysitting Terrorists: Should States Be Strictly Liable for Frailing to Prevent Transborder Attacks?*, 23 Berkely J. Int'l L. 615, 643-53 (2005).

The Chinese government has attempted to solve the attribution problem through a series of laws requiring that Internet users be able to be identified.[292] These laws include mandatory registration requirements, requirements on ISPs to track users' activity, and regulation of cyber cafes.[293] These steps have resulted in a general feeling among the Chinese people that everything they say and do on the Internet can be attributed back to them.[294] Even if these legal attempts of eliminating anonymity on the Internet were successful, it is highly unlikely they could be implemented in the western world for constitutional and human rights reasons.[295]

If attribution is a problem that cannot be eliminated entirely, for a variety of reasons, governments will not be able to rely upon deterrence as a primary means of prevention. So what strategies can be implemented to assist in the ultimate goal of preventing cyber-terrorist attacks? To help answer this question, this section now turns to current cyber and terrorism laws to determine their applicability in helping to deter cyber-terrorism.

B. Current Domestic Law Relating to Cyber-Crimes

The intent of this section is to review current laws drafted for, or commonly applied to, cyber-crimes to determine their applicability to cyber-terrorism. These statutes are not

---

[292] Marc Rotenberg, Planning for the Future of Cyber Attack Attribution, Hearing before the House of Representatives Committee on Science and Technology and Subcommittee on Technology and Innovation 2 (Jul. 15, 2010) (available at http://scholarship.law.georgetown.edu/cgi/viewcontent.cgi?article=1106&context=cong) (reviewing Chinese Internet laws relating to attribution and arguing they would be found unconstitutional is implemented in the United States).

[293] Id.

[294] Id. at 4.

[295] *See generally* Rotenberg, supra note 292.

intended as an exhaustive list of cyber related crimes, but rather those with the most potential to apply to cyber-terrorism.

1. Computer Fraud and Abuse Act (18 U.S.C. §1030)

The current domestic foundation for cyber crimes is the CFAA. Originally enacted to protect computers with a federal interest, it established criminal liability for the use of computers to commit trespass, make threats to others, damage computers, commit espionage, and the use of computers as instruments of fraud.[296] The act was broadened significantly through several amendments,[297] eventually protecting:

> computers in which there is a federal interest--federal computers, bank computers, and computers used in or effecting interstate and foreign commerce. It shields them from trespassing, threats, damage, espionage, and from being corruptly used as instruments of fraud.[298]

Given that any computer likely to be affected by an act of cyber-terrorism will somehow be involved in interstate commerce, including any computer on the Internet, the CFAA effectively has blanket applicability.

There are seven distinct crimes outlawed by the CFAA.[299] Although not originally intended as an anti-terrorism statute, the Uniting and Strengthening America by Providing Appropriate Tools Required to Intercept and Obstruct Terrorism Act of 2001 (Patriot Act) added two of the below provisions to the list of offenses that, if violated in conjunction

---

[296] *See generally* Greg Pollaro, *Disloyal Computer Use And The Computer Fraud And Abuse Act: Narrowing The Scope,* 2010 Duke L. & Tech. Rev. 12 (2010).

[297] Id. at 8.

[298] Charles Doyle, Cong. Research Serv., RL971025, Cybercrime: An Overview of the Federal Computer Fraud and Abuse Statute and Related Federal Criminal Laws 5 (2010).

[299] 18 U.S.C. §1030(a) (2006).

with a political purpose and certain violent effects, meet the definition of a federal crime of terrorism.[300] This section discusses those provisions below, but also reviews some of the CFAA provisions to see how they may be used as measures to combat acts of cyber-terrorism on their own. Section C, below, will discuss the implications of the federal crime of terrorism.

§1030(a)(1) prohibits unauthorized access to a computer to obtain national security related information, including restricted nuclear data, and using it to harm the United States or aid an enemy of the United States. The provision essentially prohibits cyber-espionage. Although I do not include strict espionage in my definition of cyber-terrorism, because by nature it is clandestine and does not produce fear or anxiety in the populace, this statute is one of the two provisions under §2332B that can rise to the level of a federal crime of terrorism. The substantial penalties for a first time offense, up to ten years imprisonment, could make this subsection an effective statute to prosecute under, if an attack can be attributed.[301]

§1030(a)(2) applies to almost any crime involving computers, as it prohibits intentionally accessing a computer without authorization or exceeding the user's authorized access to obtain information from any protected computer. The statute does require a showing that the subject has obtained information, but this is of little import as the Senate Report accompanying §1030(a)(2) states "the Committee wishes to make clear that 'obtaining information' in this context includes mere observation of the data."[302] The penalties under this §1030(a)(2) are normally misdemeanors that can be charged as

---

[300] 18 U.S.C. § 2332B (2006).
[301] 18 U.S.C. §1030(c) (2006).
[302] S. Rep No. 99-432 (1986), reprinted in 1986 U.S.C.C.A.N. 2479, 2484.

felonies with up to a five-year sentence if "the offense was committed in furtherance of any criminal or tortious act...."[303] This statute could be used effectively against organizations with terrorists aspirations conducting smaller scale or preparatory CNA for a larger attack.

§1030(a)(3) applies to unauthorized access of U.S. government computers. Although this limits the applicability of the statute, it is a simple trespass statute, not requiring that the defendant obtain any information in the commission of the crime. Therefore, if the plot of a cyber-terrorist involved access to a government computer, and if caught while exploring that computer for vulnerabilities, this statute could apply. The downside to this law is that it is a misdemeanor, unless the defendant has a prior §1030 conviction.[304] §1030(a)(2-3) could be used in a manner similar to "spitting on the sidewalk" offenses used to combat traditional terrorism.[305]

§1030(a)(5) deals with computer misuse that results in damage to the protected computer. This is the most likely statute to be used following an actual event of cyber-terrorism. It has the advantage of being very broad in scope, and has provisions for increasing penalties when certain harms are caused by the CNA, penalties reaching up to 20 years imprisonment or life depending on the effects of the attack.[306] Additionally, a

---

[303] 18 U.S.C. §1030(c)(2)(B) (2006).

[304] 18 U.S.C. §1030(c)(2) (2006).

[305] Amy Goldstein, *A Deliberate Strategy of Disruption; Massive, Secretive Detention Effort Aimed Mainly at Preventing More Terror*, Wash. Post (Nov. 4, 2001), at A1 (discussing in part Attorney General Ashcroft's use of minor crimes to prevent or investigate terrorist crimes. Ashcroft stated "Robert Kennedy's Justice Department, it is said, would arrest mobsters spitting on the sidewalk if it would help in the battle against organized crime").

[306] 18 U.S.C. §1030(c)(4) (2006). If the attack causes serious bodily injury, then the penalty is 20 years imprisonment, if death occurs as a result of the attack the penalties range up to life imprisonment.

violation of §1030(a)(5)(A) if one "knowingly causes the transmission of a program, information, code, or command, and as a result of such conduct, intentionally causes damage without authorization, to a protected computer," also falls under the §2332B terrorism statute if one of the following elements is met under §1030(c)(4)(A)(i)(II)-(VI): (II) the modification or impairment, or potential modification or impairment, of the medical examination, diagnosis, treatment, or care of 1 or more individuals; (III) physical injury to any person; (IV) a threat to public health or safety; (V) damage affecting a computer used by or for an entity of the United States Government in furtherance of the administration of justice, national defense, or national security; or (VI) damage affecting 10 or more protected computers during any 1-year period. Of particular interest is subsection (V), which would make most attacks on government websites a terrorist act. Additionally, subsection (VI) virtually ensures that any active hacking group is now guilty of terrorism.

§1030(a)(7) deals with the use of computers for extortion and transmitting threats. This could be useful in combatting organizations that threaten acts of cyber-terrorism, but without enough evidence to link them to any particular attacks.

Overall, the CFAA provides a wide range of tools for law enforcement to charge crimes against organizations seeking to commit acts of cyber-terrorism. When viewed through the lens of prevention, its main use may be at going after groups that intelligence suggest may be future cyber-terrorism threats before they acquire the capabilities to pull off such an attack. The expansive penalties possible under §1030(a)(5) do serve to effectively criminalize and punish any act of cyber-terrorism (unless seeking the death penalty). However, the CFAA is still a very traditional criminal law. It is focused on after the fact prosecution for particular instances of misconduct where each act can be attributed to an actor. The CFAA only prevents future misconduct through deterrence, which, as previously discussed, is currently inadequate in the cyber environment. Additional laws must be enacted that go to the heart of prevention, not after the fact prosecution.

2. Access Device Fraud (18 U.S.C. §1029)

Section 1029, "Fraud and related activity in connection with access devices," outlaws the "production, use, possession, or trafficking of unauthorized or counterfeit access devices."[307] The DOJ manual on Prosecuting Computer Crimes recommends using the statute to prosecute those employing "phishing" emails to obtain passwords and financial information.[308] This could be a useful statute in going after groups who are suspected of intending to commit acts of cyber-terrorism. Gaining access to computer systems would likely be an initial step in the development of any scheme of cyber-terrorism.

C. Domestic Counter-Terrorism Law Relating to Cyber-Terrorism

In addition to laws pertaining to cyber-crimes specifically, a number of laws used to prosecute terrorism offenses may also be relevant to cyber-terrorism. This section examines those laws to determine their applicability.

---

[307] 18 U.S.C. §1029(a) (2006).
[308] Office of Legal Education, U.S. Attorneys Office, Prosecuting Computer Crimes 102 (2d ed. 2010).

1. The Federal Crime of Terrorism

The federal crime of terrorism is defined as the combination of a violation of offenses listed in § 2332B(g)(5)(B), and when that violation "is calculated to influence or affect the conduct of government by intimidation or coercion, or to retaliate against government conduct."[309] There are several implications to being categorized as a federal crime of terrorism, including: an increased statute of limitations,[310] increased maximum term of supervised release,[311] and a presumption against release on bail.[312]

Being listed as a federal crime of terrorism adds some important tools for prosecutors that could assist in prevention of a cyber-terrorism event. Being able to request supervised release for life instead of five years may help prevent someone convicted for the first time of the predicate offenses from being able to strike in a more significant manner the second time around. Prevention of bail for a defendant suspected on trying to launch a cyber-terrorism attack may also help prevent an attack in its early stages. Perhaps more importantly, however, is the increased profile such attacks could achieve if they are classified as terrorism. Additionally significant is that these CFAA violations included as predicate offenses in §2332B(g)(5)(B) are also included as predicate offenses in the material support to terrorism statute.

---

[309] 18 U.S.C. § 2332B(g)(5) (2006).
[310] 18 U.S.C. § 3583 (2006). From the typical 5 years to 8 years.
[311] Id. From 5 years to life.
[312] 18 U.S.C. § 3143(e) (2006). Charles Doyle, Cong. Research Serv., RL971025, Cybercrime: An Overview of the Federal Computer Fraud and Abuse Statute and Related Federal Criminal Laws 38 (2010).

2. Material Support to Terrorism Statutes

One of the most successful legal methods in combatting terrorism, at least in terms

of prosecutions, has been the use of the material support statutes.[313] These laws work well

as a prevention method because they work to stop the flow of resources to terrorists,

hampering terrorist organizations' ability to carry out attacks. Outlawing material support

to terrorists is comprised primarily of two statutes: 18 U.S.C. §§ 2339A and 2339B

(2006). Section 2339A outlaws providing material support or resources knowing that

support is to be used in the carrying out of a violation of certain offenses deemed to rise

to the level of terrorism. Section 2339B outlaws providing any support or resources to a

designated terrorist organization. I will look at them individually to determine their

applicability to cyber-terrorism.

Section 2339A is applicable in two situations. First, if a computer were used to

effectuate a crime that is listed as a qualifying violation under the statute.[314] Thus,

providing computer training or support to a group, knowing they intend to use that

training to prepare for or perform an act of terrorism would be a crime punishable up to

15 years. More directly relevant is the second situation. Two CFAA provisions are

incorporated as predicate offenses into § 2339A. Included is "any offense listed in section

---

[313] Center on Law and Security, *Ten Years Later: Terrorist Trial Report Card 2001-2011*,
13 (2011) available at http://www.lawandsecurity.org/Publications/Terrorism-Trial-
Report-Card (listing 18 U.S.C. §§2339A & 2339B as the second and third most
prosecuted terrorism related offenses, after 18 U.S.C. § 371, Conspiracy. Since 2009,
§§2339A & 2339B have been the first and second most prosecuted offenses).
[314] The provisions included are §§ 32, 37, 81, 175, 229, 351, 831, 842 (m) or (n), 844 (f)
or (i), 930 (c), 956, 1091, 1114, 1116, 1203, 1361, 1362, 1363, 1366, 1751, 1992, 2155,
2156, 2280, 2281, 2332, 2332a, 2332b, 2332f, 2340A, or 2442 of title 18, § 236 of the
Atomic Energy Act of 1954 (42 U.S.C. § 2284), § 46502 or 60123 (b) of title 49, or any
offense listed in § 2332b (g)(5)(B) (except for sections 2339A and 2339B) or in
preparation for, or in carrying out, the concealment of an escape from the commission of
any such violation, or attempts or conspires to do such an act.

§ 2332B(g)(5)(B)," which, as seen above, includes § 1030(a)(1), and § 1030(a)(5)(A).

Therefore, providing any kind of material support, defined as:

> any property, tangible or intangible, or service, including currency or monetary
> instruments or financial securities, financial services, lodging, training, expert
> advice or assistance, safehouses, false documentation or identification,
> communications equipment, facilities, weapons, lethal substances, explosives,
> personnel (1 or more individuals who may be or include oneself), and
> transportation, except medicine or religious materials,[315]

knowing that this support will be used in the preparation for or carrying out of an act of
cyber-espionage or computer damage with certain public safety related consequences, is
prohibited and carries penalties up to 15 years imprisonment or life if death results.

§ 2339B prohibits providing material support to designated foreign terrorist
organizations (FTO). Under this statute, there is no requirement that the person providing
material support know that the support is to be used in carrying out terrorist activities.[316]
Additionally, financial institutions who become aware that they have control over
accounts of a designated FTO or its agent, must freeze those funds and report to the
Secretary of State.[317] A FTO may be so designated if the Secretary of State finds that 1)
the organization is foreign based, 2) the organization engages in terrorist activity, and 3)
this activity threatens the security of the United States or its nationals.[318] Terrorist activity

---

[315] 18 USC § 2339A(b)(1) (2006).
[316] 18 U.S.C. § 2339B(a)(1) (2006).
[317] 18 U.S.C. § 2339B(a)(2) (2006).
[318] 8 U.S.C. § 1189B(a)(1) (2006).

is primarily defined as premeditated, politically motivated violence perpetrated against noncombatant targets by subnational groups or clandestine agents.[319]

This statute has the obvious advantage of only requiring that the supporter knowingly provide support. There is no requirement, as in §2339A, of knowing the support is to be used to carry out terrorism. This makes it much easier to prosecute and therefore serves as a much greater deterrent to those who would provide support to a terrorist organization.

The downside of this statute, when looking at preventing cyber-terrorism, is two-fold. First, there is a requirement that the organization be foreign based. It can be difficult to define whether a cyber-terrorist organization is foreign or domestic, given the lack of physical infrastructure required to maintain the organization. No training camps are required, and the members do not even need to reside in the same place. However, this could cut both ways, as almost every hacking organization is, at least in part, foreign.

Second, the definition of terrorist activity is unclear as to whether it would include cyber-terrorism. It does not explicitly mention CNA, and the statute's definition of terrorism requires "violence." As previously discussed, CNA may result in fear and anxiety among the populace without producing violent effects. This is inconsistent with CNA included in the federal crime of terrorism, which does not require violent effects.[320]

Looking at the two material support statutes, it is unclear how much utility they would have in combatting cyber-terrorism. CNA is clearly included in § 2339A, but the applicability to § 2339B is much less clear. I will discuss in Section VII how the material

---

[319] 22 U.S.C. § 2656f(d)(2) (2006).
[320] 18 U.S.C. § 2332B (2006).

support statutes can be amended to make them a more valuable tool in preventing cyber-terrorism.

3. Specially Designated Global Terrorist under EO 13224

In addition to designated FTOs, under Executive Order 13224 and related regulations the executive branch can label terrorist groups, individuals acting as part of a terrorist organization, and other entities providing financial support or assistance, as a Specially Designated Global Terrorist (SDGT).[321] The Secretary of State, in consultation with the Secretary of the Treasury and the Attorney General, may designate foreign individuals or entities determined to have committed, or pose a significant risk of committing, acts of terrorism that threaten the security of U.S. nationals or the national security, foreign policy, or economy of the U.S.[322] Additionally, the Secretary of the Treasury, in consultation with the Secretary of State and the Attorney General, may designate as "Specially Designated Nationals" (SDNs), individuals or entities that are determined: 1) To be owned or controlled by, or act for or on behalf of an individual or entity so designated; 2) To assist in, sponsor, or provide financial, material, or technological support for acts of terrorism or individuals or entities so designated; or 3) To be otherwise associated with certain individuals or entities designated in or under the Order. Most SDGTs and SDNs are foreign persons, but the late Anwar al-Awlaki, a U.S. Person, was designated as an SDGT.[323]

---

[321] U.S. Dep't of State, Office of the Spokesman, *Foreign Terrorist Organization Designation Fact Sheet* (Sept. 1, 2010), http://www.state.gov/r/pa/prs/ps/2010/09/146554.htm.

[322] Exec. Order No. 13,224, 66 Fed. Reg. 49079 (Sept. 25, 2001).

[323] Office of Foreign Assets Control, *Specially Designated National and Blocked Persons List* 36, http://www.treasury.gov/ofac/downloads/t11sdn.pdf (last accessed Feb. 6, 2012).

EO 13224 defines terrorism as an activity that involves "a violent act or an act dangerous to human life, property, or infrastructure; and appears to be intended to intimidate or coerce a civilian population, influence the policy of a government by intimidation or coercion, or affect the conduct of a government by mass destruction, assassination, kidnaping, or hostage-taking."[324] Here the applicability to cyber-terrorism depends upon the interpretation of "an act dangerous to human life, property, or infrastructure." If data is considered property, and information systems are considered infrastructure, then the EO could certainly apply to cyber-terrorism. This ambiguity, however, could serve to inhibit the use of this tool in preventing cyber-terrorism.

4. Conspiracy

There are two conspiracy statutes directly applicable to cyber-terrorism: 18 U.S.C. § 371, conspiracy to commit an offense or to defraud the United States; and 18 U.S.C. § 956, conspiracy to kill, kidnap, maim, or injure persons or damage property in a foreign country. Although not applying directly to terrorism, Section 371 was the most charged statute relating to terrorist crimes in the ten years following 9/11.[325] Given that any act of cyber-terrorism is covered, at a minimum, under the CFAA, there are no obstacles in using § 371 to combat cyber-terrorism.

If, however, the DoJ chooses to use Section 956 to charge a group conspiring to commit an act of cyber-terrorism in a foreign country, the statute is less than clear. Section 956(b) criminalizes any conspiracy:

---

[324] Exec. Order 13224 § 3(d).
[325] Center on Law and Security, *Ten Years Later: Terrorist Trial Report Card 2001-2011*, 13 (2011) available at http://www.lawandsecurity.org/Publications/Terrorism-Trial-Report-Card.

to damage or destroy specific property situated within a foreign country and

belonging to a foreign government or to any political subdivision thereof with

which the United States is at peace, or any railroad, canal, bridge, airport, airfield,

or other public utility, public conveyance, or public structure, or any religious,

educational, or cultural property so situated.

This statute is focused on property belonging to foreign governments and certain

segments of infrastructure. It is unclear whether damage to the data contained on

information systems would apply.

Part V. Incorporating Cyber-Terrorism into Current Law

"Better to be despised for too anxious apprehensions, than ruined by too confident

security." - Edmund Burke, Reflections on the Revolution in France

Part IV examined the applicability of current cyber-crime and counter-terror law to

counter-terrorism. This examination revealed several important gaps in those laws that

might prevent their use in the fight against cyber-terrorism. The previous section also

found that these laws do not provide an adequate focus on the prevention of cyber-

terrorism. To help remedy this, part V proposes that this paper's definition of cyber-

terrorism be incorporated into some of the most frequently used laws to combat terrorism,

thereby filling those gaps and providing tools to law enforcement for the prevention of

cyber-terrorism.

A. Material Support to Terrorism Statutes

As previously discussed, the material support statutes have proven some of the

most effective tools in the counter-terrorism toolkit. The Department of Justice (DoJ) has

referred to the material support to terrorism statutes[326] as "[o]ne of the cornerstones of

our prosecution efforts" in the battle against terrorism.[327] In explaining the effectiveness

of the statutes, the DoJ quoted a defendant, who made the following statement in

conversation with an informant:[328]

---

[326] These statutes include 18 U.S.C. §§ 2339A & 2339B, as well as 50 U.S.C. § 1701 et
seq.
[327] U.S. Dep't of Justice, Counterterrorism White Paper, June 22, 2006, at 14.
[328] Id. at 15.

[T]he reason it was not organized is, couldn't be organized as it should've been, is

because we don't have support. Everybody's scared to give up any money to help

us. You know what I'm saying? Because of the law that Bush wrote about, you

know, supporting terrorism whatever the whole thing. ... Everybody's scared ...

[Bush] made a law that say, for instance, I left out of the country and I fought,

right, but I wasn't able to afford a ticket but you bought my plane ticket, you gave

me the money to do it ... By me going and me fighting and doing that they can, by

this new law, they can come and take you and put you in jail for supporting what

they call terrorism.

Given the success of this tool, its full potential should be utilized in countering cyber-

terrorism.[329] The gaps previously identified in § 2339B[330] should be remedied to fully

allow for designations of cyber-terrorist organizations. The two main problems are the

definitions of terrorism,[331] and the requirement that designated organizations be

foreign.[332]

The first step is incorporating cyber-terrorism into the definition of terrorism as

used in the statute regarding designation of a FTO: "premeditated, politically motivated

violence perpetrated against noncombatant targets by subnational groups or clandestine

---

[329] As discussed supra, cyber-terrorism is covered under § 2339A by incorporating provisions of the CFAA as predicate offenses.

[330] What is less certain, is whether a cyber-terrorist organization could be designated as a FTO by the Secretary of State, as applied under § 2339B.

[331] 22 U.S.C. § 2656F(d)(2) (2006).

[332] To be designated as a FTO, the organization in question must meet the following requirements: 1) the organization is a foreign organization; 2) the organization engages in terrorist activity; and 3) the terrorist activity or terrorism of the organization threatens the security of United States nationals or the national security of the United States. 8 U.S.C. § 1189 (2006).

agents."[333] The violence requirement effectively precludes many potential acts of cyber-terrorism, as previously discussed. If the proposed definition of cyber-terrorism were included along with the definition of terrorism, the Secretary of State could then designate foreign organizations that engage in cyber-terrorist activity. However, identifying cyber-terrorist organizations as foreign is difficult due to the attribution dilemma. Hacker organizations such as Anonymous and Lulz are worldwide with no specific locus.[334]

Given the issue of identifying the precise locus of cyber-terrorist organizations, 8 U.S.C. § 1189 should also be amended with respect to cyber-terrorist organizations and the definition of "foreign organizations."[335] If the phrase were changed to "the organization is a foreign organization or conducts operations primarily through cyberspace," it would resolve the difficult question of whether a cyber-terrorist group is foreign or not. The inevitable question is why include domestic cyber-terrorist groups, but not other terrorist organizations? Given the problem of attribution and tracking an organization that operates in cyberspace, an exception should be made. A cyber-terrorist group may operate from different locations around the world with no specific physical center and may include both domestic and foreign members.

Another counter to this proposal is that outlawing material support would have little effect in stopping a cyber-terrorist organization. Preventing the flow of money and training to a group of advanced computer hackers will not hinder operations the way it does to a traditional terrorist group that needs to travel, needs weapons, and needs a base

---

[333] 22 U.S.C. § 2656F(d)(2) (2006).
[334] *See* Keating, *supra* note 157.
[335] 8 U.S.C. § 1189 (2006).

of operations. However, one only need look to an example of an advanced cyber-weapon to counter this theory. Stuxnet, the malware that did so much damage to the Iranian nuclear centrifuges, was estimated to have cost $1 million to produce, and probably needed the backing of nation states.[336] If the definition of cyber-terrorism is limited to only those major attacks with serious effects, then it is false to say that these attacks would not require some level of financial and logistical support.

B. Amend FISA's definition of international terrorism

The Foreign Intelligence Surveillance Act (FISA) was not passed as a counter-terrorism tool, but rather as a means to collect intelligence on foreign powers. However, with the rise of international terrorist organizations in the last two decades, and amendments such as "lone wolf" provision,[337] FISA has become an important counter-terrorism tool. FISA's increased importance over the last decade is revealed in the rising number of FISA warrants granted. In 1998, barely 800 FISA warrants were granted.[338] By 2008, that number was over 2000.[339] The ability to electronically survey those suspected of terror is valuable to both prevent terrorist activities and lead law enforcement to those who support terrorism. FISA would be particularly useful against organizations that

---

[336] Ben Flanagan, *Former CIA chief speaks out on Iran Stuxnet attack*, The National, Dec. 15, 2011, http://www.thenational.ae/thenationalconversation/industry-insights/technology/former-cia-chief-speaks-out-on-iran-stuxnet-attack (referring to statements by Gen. Michael Hayden, former head of the National Security Agency).
[337] 50 U.S.C. § 1801(b)(1)(C) (2006).
[338] Report from Janet Reno, Attorney General of the U.S., to Hon. Dennis Hastert, Speaker of the U.S. House of Representatives (Apr. 29, 1999), *available at* http://www.fas.org/irp/agency/doj/fisa/1998rept.html.
[339] Report from Ronald Weich, Assistant Attorney General of the U.S., to Hon. Harry Reid, Majority Leader of the U.S. Senate (May 14, 2009), *available at* http://www.fas.org/irp/agency/doj/fisa/2008rept.pdf.

operate primarily in the electronic realm, and therefore should be expanded to ensure it covers cyber-terrorism.

FISA allows for the electronic surveillance of a foreign power for the purpose of collecting intelligence information within the United States without a Title III warrant.[340] Included in the definition of a foreign power under the statute are groups "engaged in international terrorism or activities in preparation therefor."[341] Also included as an "agent of a foreign power" under the statute is the so-called lone-wolf provision. This provision includes "any person other than a United States person, who engages in international terrorism or activities in preparation therefore."[342] However, FISA's definition of "international terrorism" includes the following phrase: "activities that involve violent acts or acts dangerous to human life."[343] Again, this definition is ambiguous when it comes to applying cyber-terrorism. It could exclude a group's conducting cyber-terrorism through a non-violent attack, such as destruction of financial or national security data.

FISA should be amended to include as a foreign power groups "engaged in international terrorism, cyber-terrorism, or activities in preparation thereof." The lone wolf provision should also be amended to include cyber-terrorism in a similar way. Adding cyber-terrorism to the definition of international terrorism included in FISA would be an important step in adding FISA as an effective tool to prevent cyber-terrorism.

---

[340] 50 U.S.C. § 1802 (2006).
[341] 50 U.S.C. § 1801(a)(4) (2006).
[342] 50 U.S.C. § 1801(b)(1)(C) (2006).
[343] 50 U.S.C. § 1801(c)(1) (2006).

C. Conspiracy

As discussed in the previous section, using 18 U.S.C. § 956, conspiracy to kill, kidnap, maim, or injure persons or damage property in a foreign country, is defined as follows:

> to damage or destroy specific property situated within a foreign country and belonging to a foreign government or to any political subdivision thereof with which the United States is at peace, or any railroad, canal, bridge, airport, airfield, or other public utility, public conveyance, or public structure, or any religious, educational, or cultural property so situated.

Using this statute against cyber-terrorism is problematic because it is unclear if the phrase "to damage or destroy specific property" or "other public utility" would include damage to data contained in information systems.

This statute could be remedied to more clearly cover cyber-terrorism in two different ways, one broad and one narrow. The broad solution would be to include "information systems related both to foreign governments and operation of the included infrastructure components" in the litany of included targets. This inclusion, however, would include minor CNA, such as denial of service attacks. This would violate the serious intent of this particular statute.

The narrow solution would be to add a clause to § 956; amending it to read: "to damage or destroy specific property through any physical means or act of cyber-terrorism, situated within a foreign country and belonging to a foreign government or to any political subdivision thereof with which the United States is at peace, or any railroad, canal, bridge, airport, airfield, economic data system, or other public utility, utility control

system, public conveyance, or public structure, or any religious, educational, or cultural

property so situated." This clause would criminalize an act of cyber-terrorism, as defined

by this paper, directed against a foreign countries economic systems or infrastructure

control systems, such as a SCADA control. This would be narrower than the first option

in that it significantly narrows the qualifying types of CNA that rise to the level of cyber-

terrorism.

D. Weapons of Mass Destruction

As seen with the Stuxnet virus, cyber-weapons can potentially result in effects on the

same level as weapons of mass destruction (WMD). Although WMD are often thought of

as chemical, biological, radiological, and nuclear weapons (referred to by the acronym

CBRN), the definition under 18 U.S.C. § 2332A of a WMD is much broader. Along with

the CBRN type weapons, the statute includes a wide variety of destructive devices as

defined under 18 U.S.C. § 921, including bombs and grenades. Thus, a WMD is not as

narrow a category as often thought in the public conscience. However nowhere in

§ 2332A, or in the WMD definition under the FISA,[344] is CNA included unless it were to

cause a release of chemical, biological, or radiological substance.

Despite this lack of statutory inclusion, there are warnings that cyber-weapons could

be another form of WMD. As recently as January 2009, former Director of National

Intelligence (DNI) Mike McConnell equated "cyber weapons" with WMD when he

expressed concern about terrorists' use of technology to degrade the nation's

---

[344] 50 U.S.C. § 1801(p) (2006).

infrastructure.[345] Director McConnell noted that terrorists aim to damage infrastructure and that the "time is not too far off when the level of sophistication reaches a point that there could be strategic damage to the United States."[346]

This exclusion could be easily remedied by adding cyber weapons designed to cause cyber-terrorism (as defined by this paper) to the statutes including WMD in the U.S. Code. It should again be stressed, that this definition is designed to exclude all but the most serious CNA from its scope. By incorporating these types of weapons into the definition of WMD, any use of that cyber-weapon by or against a national of the United States is criminalized.[347] This amendment would also bring an extra-territorial statute into the legal arsenal of law enforcement and help address the jurisdictional dilemma posed by CNA. Incorporating this definition into the FISA would bring those who develop or proliferate in cyber-terrorism weapons under the jurisdiction of the FISA.[348]

---

[345] The Charlie Rose Show, "Interview of Mr. Mike McConnell, Director of National Intelligence," PBS (Jan. 8, 2009).
[346] Id.
[347] 50 U.S.C. § 2332A (2006).
[348] 50 U.S.C. § 1801 (2006).

Conclusion

From hacktivists who wish to make a political point by temporarily altering websites,[349] to foreign governments and corporations wishing to steal valuable intellectual property,[350] to common criminals wishing to steal credit card information for financial gain,[351] the motivations behind CNA are almost as broad as the uses of the Internet. Given the broad range of CNA, the tendency has been to seek legal responses that cover these crimes as a whole. Just as non-Internet related activities such as espionage, theft of intellectual property, financial crimes, and terrorism have each developed unique legal regimes to deal with the particularities of each crime, so have different types of cyber-crimes. However, a notable exception is cyber-terrorism, which has yet to be defined in the U.S. Code.

Despite certain sections of the CFAA being listed as predicate offenses in the federal crime of terrorism, the resulting applicability is narrow and does little to address the prevention of cyber-terrorism. As terrorist organizations become more sophisticated in the field of information technology, it will only be a matter of time before they attempt

---

[349] Molly Wood, *Anonymous goes nuclear; everybody loses?*, CNET.com (Jan. 19, 2012 5:40 PM), http://news.cnet.com/8301-31322_3-57362437-256/anonymous-goes-nuclear-everybody-loses/ (discussing the hacktivist group Anonymous' takedown of several government websites, include the FBI and DOJ, following the arrest of several executives associated with megaupload.com, a file-sharing site).

[350] Nicole Perlroth, *Hacked Chamber of Commerce Opposed Cybersecurity Law*, N.Y. Times Bits Blog (Dec. 21, 2011 6:10 PM), http://bits.blogs.nytimes.com/2011/12/21/hacked-chamber-of-commerce-opposed-cybersecurity-law/ (reporting on US Chamber of Commerce claims that sensitive economic data was accessed during a CNA originating in China).

[351] Matt Richtel, *Credit Card Theft is Thriving Online as Global Market*, N.Y. Times (May. 13, 2002), http://www.nytimes.com/2002/05/13/business/credit-card-theft-is-thriving-online-as-global-market.html?scp=2&sq=online+credit+card+theft&st=nyt (noting that tens of thousands of credit card numbers are offered for sale every week on the Internet).

to conduct terrorist activities through information systems. These attacks could be broad based denial of service attacks such as the attacks on Estonia, or they could be narrow malware attacks on SCADA systems, such as the Stuxnet virus in Iran.

There has not been a cyber-terrorist event as of yet in the United States, but this should not stop Congress from drafting legislation to help prevent cyber-terrorism in the United States and abroad. The first step in any such legislation must be a careful definition of cyber-terrorism. This paper proposes a definition that is at once broad enough to cover the potentially unique effects of a weapon of cyber-terrorism, while narrow enough to exclude computer network attacks that are relatively minor in nature, for a definition that is either too broad or too narrow risks being either irrelevant or useless.

Once a proper definition is arrived at, it can be incorporated into existing legislation developed in the fight against traditional terrorism. Material support statutes, the FISA, conspiracy, and WMD statutes all hold potential in preventing cyber-terrorism, but must first incorporate cyber-terrorism into their definitions and coverage. A formal legal definition will also allow various government agencies to operate from a common standard in developing tactics, techniques and procedures for countering cyber-terrorism.

These steps will obviously not provide all the tools needed to stop cyber-terrorists. Increased cyber-security aimed at government and critical infrastructure information systems and greater information sharing are also important requirements in stopping cyber-terrorists. Potential laws aimed at requiring widespread use of data encryption also hold potential for stopping would be cyber-terrorists. But just as the fight against terrorism has left no stone unturned in finding ways to defeat terrorists, so should the fight against cyber-terrorists. The fact that there has not yet been a "cyber 9/11" should

not deter government taking the extremely important steps of defining the problem and

using the definition to amend existing counter-terrorism statutes.